Decoding Your
DREAMS

DECODING YOUR
DREAMS

What the Lord May Be Saying
to You While You Sleep

JENNIFER LeCLAIRE

EMANATE
BOOKS

Published in Nashville, Tennessee, by Emanate Books, an imprint of Thomas Nelson. Emanate Books and Thomas Nelson are registered trademarks of HarperCollins Christian Publishing, Inc.

Thomas Nelson titles may be purchased in bulk for educational, business, fund-raising, or sales promotional use. For information, please e-mail SpecialMarkets@ThomasNelson.com.

Scripture quotations marked CEV are from the Contemporary English Version. Copyright © 1991, 1992, 1995 by American Bible Society. Used by permission.

Scripture quotations marked GNT are from the Good News Translation in Today's English Version— Second Edition. Copyright 1992 by American Bible Society. Used by permission.

Scripture quotations marked NASB are from New American Standard Bible®. Copyright © 1960, 1962, 1963, 1968, 1971, 1972, 1973, 1975, 1977, 1995 by The Lockman Foundation. Used by permission. (www.Lockman.org)

Scripture quotations marked NIV are from the Holy Bible, New International Version®, NIV®. Copyright © 1973, 1978, 1984, 2011 by Biblica, Inc.® Used by permission of Zondervan. All rights reserved worldwide. www.Zondervan.com. The "NIV" and "New International Version" are trademarks registered in the United States Patent and Trademark Office by Biblica, Inc.®

Scripture quotations marked NLT are from the Holy Bible, New Living Translation. © 1996, 2004, 2007, 2013, 2015 by Tyndale House Foundation. Used by permission of Tyndale House Publishers, Inc., Carol Stream, Illinois 60188. All rights reserved.

Scripture quotations marked NKJV are taken from the New King James Version®. © 1982 by Thomas Nelson. Used by permission. All rights reserved.

Scripture quotations marked KJV are taken from the King James Version. Public domain.

ISBN 978-0-7852-2354-2 (eBook)
ISBN 978-0-7852-2353-5 (TP)

Library of Congress Control Number: 2018943316

Printed in the United States of America
HB 04.01.2024

I dedicate this book to the pioneers of dream interpretation, the men who taught me the most about decoding God's dreams—James Goll and the late John Paul Jackson. Although they taught about dreams from different perspectives, these men of God paved the way for an open understanding and accurate representation of how God speaks to us in our dreams—and how to decode what He is saying.

CONTENTS

CONTENTS

FOREWORD

Many of us find ourselves floating down the fast-paced current of the river of God never allowing ourselves the time needed to find the shore where we can pause to ponder on the mysteries of God's revelatory ways in our very own lives. It is into those private places that God's presence and God's word seeks to invade our lives. This is where the Master Dream Weaver appears, eager to reveal Himself to us in unique and unusual ways.

Personally, I have studied these prophetic ways of the Holy Spirit for years. I have spent time studying the three hundred Scripture references to dreams and visions in the Bible multiple times over a thirty-year period. I have read or gleaned more than 110 books on dreams from about every perspective that there is. I was exposed to the "Seer of Seers" in John Paul Jackson and Bob Jones.

Then I had my own dream explosion that took place in my own life. Journals? Oh yes, I have journaled. These journals contain a lot of experience, trial and error, and loads of crazy and amazing stuff that still leaves me pondering. That is what dreams do. That is what dreamers do. They make you inquire of God! Oh the joy of the never-ending classes you can take in the School of the Holy Spirit!

Next Generation of Prophetic Dreamers

Having had the benefit of hanging out with the Seers and Naba prophets both, I always have my eyeballs open for the next generation of prophetic dreamers. Many new voices are quickly emerging on the scene. Now appears Jennifer LeClaire, a dreamer in her generation. Yes, here comes another dreamer of God's big dreams.

Jennifer now picks up the baton that others and I have carried. In this distinct book, she now comes alongside to help you build a framework to enable you to understand the work of this Master Weaver in your personal dream life.

Like a spiritual Indiana Jones, you can learn to pick up your own discovery magnifying glass and find out that dreams and the interpretation of dreams is neither a modern phenomenon nor a unique event in the life of God's people. Spiritual dreams have their roots in ancient Judaism, as well as in the early church.

In fact, dreams have been the source of some of the greatest paradigm shifts in the history of Judaism and the church. Consider Abraham and Peter! The birth of Israel was spoken of as Abraham slept on the desert sands and Peter's dream opened the door of the church to the Gentile world. Through dreams God communicates with us concerning our destiny as well as the destinies of our families, our nation, and our world. And He will communicate personally straight to your life's circumstances and destiny.

Because dreams are notoriously elusive, it is important that we have some deciphering tools in our hands that will help us capture our dreams for the purpose of interpreting those dreams. What good is a spiritual dream if it is not remembered nor interpreted correctly? Sadly we would run the risk of losing God's word for our lives. I will provide those simple and yet oft considered mysterious tools so that you, too, will become a dream catcher.

But do not worry; the tools of a lost trade are being restored in these days. For behold, here comes another dreamer!

May All Your Dreams Come True!

Dr. James W. Goll
Founder of God Encounters Ministries
Author, International Speaker, and Recording Artist

INTRODUCTION

As I travel around the world teaching believers the principles of dream interpretation, I find how God communicates to us while we're sound asleep is one of the most neglected topics in the body of Christ—yet it's one of the primary ways the Lord speaks to us in the last days.

In the book of Acts, Peter re-prophesied the words the Lord spoke through the prophet Joel: "'In the last days it shall be,' says God, 'that I will pour out My Spirit on all flesh; your sons and your daughters shall prophesy, your young men shall see visions'" (Acts 2:17).

Joel and Peter weren't prophesying about soulish dreams, nightmares, or pizza dreams. The Amplified Classic translation spells out the meaning of these prophetic verses in much greater detail: "And it shall come to pass in the last days, God declares, that I will pour out of My Spirit upon all mankind, and your sons and your daughters shall prophesy [telling forth the divine counsels] and your young men shall see visions [divinely granted appearances], and your old men shall dream [divinely suggested] dreams" (Acts 2:17).

It's likely you are having "divinely suggested" dreams whether you remember them or not. This book will give you sound tips on how to remember more of those divinely suggested dreams and what to do when you know you've had a significant dream but the recall escapes you. It's also likely you are searching for answers—real answers—about what those dreams mean. Some of the dreams may frighten you. Others may intrigue you. Still others may thrill your heart, even if you don't know exactly what they mean. This book will help you navigate these and many other dream-related issues.

Although God speaks differently in dreams than He does in the still, small voice of prophecy with which we are more familiar, He wants you to understand what He is saying in every communication medium through which He decides to send you a message. Of course, the enemy knows this and is working to exploit hungry hearts. In a time when more and more Christians are reporting an increase in dreams, many curious, God-fearing believers are finding a lack of Christian expertise in this area and are turning to dream dictionaries compiled by worldly scholars or psychics.

Indeed, too many believers are being led astray by staunch dream interpretation dictionaries or, worse, New Age websites that claim to unveil the meanings of our dreams, or they turn to false prophets who will interpret dreams for a price. People are making major life decisions based on false dream interpretations and experiencing great distress. This is not the will of God.

Yes, there are solid dream dictionaries authored by Christians with the spiritual gift of dream interpretation, and I am thankful for them. I am thankful for men like the late John Paul Jackson, who did so much to open our understanding of the dream world, encouraging us to seek out the meanings of dreams. I am grateful for one of my fathers in the faith, James Goll, who has done so much to bring clarity and impart the dreamer's anointing to a generation. I am grateful for these and so many others who have labored to encourage the body of Christ to press into dreams and accurately weigh what the Lord is saying.

I encourage you to read all the books on dreams from reputable authors you can find. But I warn you, not all books about dreams in the Christian book market contain unadulterated truth. Many stray so far beyond the bounds of Scripture that there is no anchor for your faith. I caution you to be careful about books that elevate experience above Scripture. Experiences are vital and helpful in illustrating Scripture, but without Scripture to anchor the experience, we can easily veer off into error. The dream you don't judge rightly is the dream that can derail your life.

I wrote this book on dreams with a heart to provide a solid, safe explanation of the dream world and dream languages for the next generation of dreamers. My intention is that it will help readers understand what God is really saying to them. I hope to facilitate the understanding that one size does not fit all in the dream interpretation world.

You are the best interpreter of your dreams—you know best how you relate to God and how He relates to you. You will learn standard applications and "best practices" in dream interpretation throughout the pages of this book. I pray these truths also inspire you to pay attention most of all to your relationship to God and how He speaks to you, uniquely and individually, both while you are awake and while you sleep.

Happy dreaming!

> The dream you don't judge rightly is the dream that can derail your life.

Chapter 1

GOD SPEAKS THROUGH DREAMS

My First Prophetic Dream

The first time I realized God was speaking to me in a dream, I woke up perplexed—but now it makes perfect sense. In the dream I was about five months pregnant. But I wasn't married and had no reason to be pregnant. I was trying to deny it, but my mid-section was clearly swelling and it wasn't because of too many tasty empanadas from the corner Cuban café. In my dream, I asked a trusted friend what she thought. To my dismay, she said, "You're definitely pregnant!"

To say I was none too happy would be a monumental under-statement. A flood of thoughts rushed at me in my dream state. *How will I get all my work done with a newborn baby to care for? I'm too busy for this! My life is challenging enough as it is. This is certainly no time to complicate things with a baby!* Still, I knew there was no way of escaping this. I had the heavy sense that I really didn't have a choice in the matter. This baby was coming in about four months, whether I liked it or not.

Then I woke up perplexed. I'm not spiritually dense, so I understood the overarching meaning of the dream. God was birthing a new thing in my life. We were a little more than halfway through the incubation process, and I needed to align my will with His in a hurry. My fellow prophets chimed in as to what this "baby" could be. Some said it was a new ministry. Others said it would ultimately be a good thing, though times were likely to get rough during the next few months. They were all right.

It's interesting how God gives His prophets different perspectives and at times they seem almost to contradict one another, but in the end you see how they all fit together. The messianic prophecies are a good example. But I digress. Or do I? It's been almost a year since I had that dream, and since then I've had others about the baby as both an infant and a toddler. The Lord recently brought these things to my remembrance while I was reading about Mary, the human mother of Jesus, and a messianic prophecy she received that changed her life. And there's a lesson in it for us all as we approach new beginnings.

You'll remember when the angel Gabriel, often seen delivering messages to God's people, found Mary in Nazareth. Gabriel told Mary she was highly favored of the Lord and blessed among women. Then Gabriel delivered his prophetic message: "You will conceive and give birth to a son, and you are to call him Jesus" (Luke 1:31 NIV). Mary was perplexed and asked the angel how it was possible as she was a virgin.

Imagine the flood of thoughts rushing through Mary's mind. She wasn't married, so turning up pregnant would be more than a little inconvenient. Unlike my superficial complaints about finding time to get my work done with a newborn's diapers to change, Mary's prophetic revelation could have cost her everything. Not only was she in danger of losing Joseph, the love of her life, she could also end up on trial for fornication, which was reason enough to be stoned under Mosaic law. Mary probably imagined many things about her fate.

Then Gabriel answered Mary: "The Holy Ghost shall come upon thee, and the power of the Highest shall overshadow thee: therefore also that holy thing which shall be born of thee shall be called the Son of God" (Luke 1:35 KJV). Gabriel gave her two other insights. He told Mary that her cousin Elisabeth, who had been barren, was pregnant in her old age. He also told her all things were possible with God. At this news, Mary probably remembered Abraham and Sarah's miracle baby and began to put her faith in God.

"Mary responded, 'I am the Lord's servant. May everything you have said about me come true'" (Luke 1:38 NLT). Mary displayed willingness and obedience to allow the Lord to use her however He chose. I don't believe He would have used her if she had not been willing and obedient. God will not violate our own will. That's why, after I awakened from my pregnancy dream, my concern wasn't so much about receiving a revelation on exactly what I was birthing but about lining up my will with God's will in the matter.

Let's get real. Birthing anything, from a baby to a ministry to a business, is hard work. It changes your life. It forces you to become more disciplined. It challenges you to go deeper in your relationship with God to find the grace you need to survive the spiritual stretching you will no doubt experience. Indeed, birthing new things demands many adjustments. That's why so many people have aborted the call of God on their lives. It's not that they couldn't yield to the Spirit of God and work with Him to birth something new. It's that they were not willing.

I believe God is birthing new things—and He needs people who are like Mary, willing and obedient to allow the Lord to do what He pleases for His glory. Notice I say *for His glory*. Mary gave birth to Jesus not for herself, but so that the sin of the world could be taken away. Whatever the Lord chooses to birth through you—a song, a book, or an entire ministry—remember that it's not about you. It's about the people who need what you are carrying. You aren't carrying the Savior of the world, but you may very well be carrying something that will save people a lot of pain, bring people greater understanding of God's Word, or give people the hope of fulfilling their purpose and destiny in Christ. Isn't it worth it?

<hr />

Is God really speaking to you in your dreams? Could the Lord Almighty be warning you of things to come while you lie in bed at night? Is it possible the Creator of the universe is giving you innovative ideas while you sleep? Simply stated, yes. God has spoken to people through dreams since the book of Genesis, and He is still sending messages through dreams today.

Just consider some famous dreams throughout history that have advanced society. God created the atom—the basic building blocks of anything and everything—but Niels Bohr, the father of quantum mechanics, discovered these tiny particles during a dream.[1] Bohr said the revelation that laid the groundwork for the atomic model was birthed through a dream of sitting on the sun with planets "hissing around on tiny cords." Bohr's dream-state discovery paved the way for our understanding of chemistry and physics, which led to scientific and technological breakthroughs, such as lasers, night vision goggles, and digital cameras.

Likewise, Albert Einstein pointed to a dream he had as a teenager that he meditated on his whole life. "He dreamt that he was riding a sled down a steep, snowy slope and, as he approached the speed of light in his dream, the colors all blended into one," explained John W. Price in an interview on the radio show *Engines of Our Ingenuity*. "He spent much of his career, inspired by that dream, thinking about what happens at the speed of light."[2] Einstein's theory of relativity helps physicists understand optics and radio waves and sets the stage for ideas like time travel. Can you imagine?

Paul McCartney said he heard the melody for the famous Beatles song "Yesterday" in a dream. Elias Howe invented sewing machines after a dream that gave him insight into the mechanical penetration of a needle. Edgar Allan Poe's nightmares inspired some of his famous poetry, and he also penned essays about dreams because he was so fascinated with the dream world. More recently, Google founder Larry Page had a dream about "downloading the entire web onto computers" that has revolutionized the internet.

Were all these dreams from God? Probably not, but they nevertheless show you the power of dreams, and some of those dreams likely were divinely suggested. By the same token, history records significant warning dreams that may have come from God Himself. President Abraham Lincoln dreamed of his own assassination. Many people had dreams about a disaster on the *Titanic*, and some of them refused to get on board as a result. The same goes for people foreshadowing certain catastrophic events, such as 9/11, school shootings, and plane crashes.

The Bible mentions dreams and visions more than two hundred times. In the Old Testament we read about Joseph, Daniel, Jacob, Nebuchadnezzar, Solomon, and Job dreaming significant dreams. In the New Testament, the Bible records the dreams of Mary's husband Joseph, the wise men, Pilate's wife, Paul, Peter, and John. We're witnessing a radical increase of God speaking through dreams today, which is in agreement with Acts 2:17 KJV: "And it shall come to pass in the last days, saith God, I will pour out of My Spirit upon all flesh; your sons and your daughters shall prophesy, and your young men shall see visions, and your old men shall dream dreams."

God Created Us to Dream

God created us to dream. Dreaming is part of the human experience. The Bible says plenty about dreams. Understanding the Scripture truths about the dream world will serve as a foundation for everything else you learn in this book.

When Peter prophesied in Acts 2:17, he was re-prophesying what Joel originally chronicled eight hundred years earlier. Remember, these words are not Peter's words or Joel's words. This was the word of the Lord. Again, Joel chronicled it this way: "And it shall come to pass afterward that I will pour out My Spirit on all flesh; Your sons and your daughters shall prophesy, your old men shall dream dreams, your young men shall see visions."

Whether you are young or old, male or female, God created you to dream. The early Jewish culture understood this. According to *The Jewish Encyclopedia*, "The fact that the most famous teachers frequently discuss dreams and enunciate doctrines regarding them, shows the strong hold dreams had upon the minds even of the intellectual leaders of Judaism. Belief in dreams was the rule; doubt concerning them, the exception."[3]

Before you finish reading this first chapter, I pray the Word of God will build your faith in the reality that God speaks to you in dreams. Depending on what you've been taught—or haven't been taught—during your walk with Christ, it may be hard for you to believe that the Creator of the universe communicates with you while you sleep. Consider the Scriptures, meditate on them, and believe that the God of dreams can redeem your time of slumber and speak to you while you are resting your body.

The Reason God Speaks to Us in Dreams

We see clearly throughout Scripture that God does speak to His people through dreams and visions. The question is why? Why does the Creator of the universe choose to speak to us when we are in an unconscious state?

It's interesting, first of all, to explore how God moved on His people in unconscious states in Scripture. Genesis 2:21 KJV tells us, "And the LORD God caused a deep sleep to fall upon Adam, and he slept: and he took one of his ribs, and closed up the flesh instead thereof." Again, in Genesis, we read that the Lord put Abram into a deep sleep to speak to him about a covenant (15:12). Daniel fell into a deep sleep while the angel was speaking to him about the interpretation of visions from the Lord (Dan. 8:18, 10:9).

Clearly, God chooses to communicate some things to us while we are asleep. We know God gives us dreams with many purposes, such as building our faith, revealing our destiny, warning us of danger, and so on. We'll discuss different types, purposes, and categories of dreams in later chapters. But, again, why does God choose this mode of communication at certain times? He can and does speak to us in many ways. Why dreams?

I don't propose to have all the answers to this question, and I've studied to no avail hoping to find a definitive answer. I haven't yet found anyone who can answer this question with absolute scriptural backing. I can only offer wisdom from experience.

One theory is that we are too dull of hearing to catch His message while we're awake. That could be true in some cases. When our emotions are running wild, He may choose to speak to us while our souls are less distracted (during sleep) and can interpret what He is saying once we are awake and seeking.

Here's another theory: What He is showing us is too spectacular to believe with our natural minds, so God supersedes our spiritual hearing during daytime hours to deliver a visual or sensory message while we're asleep—a message we have a hard time explaining away. While we are awake, we may hear a voice and question if it is God's. Spectacular dreams or dreams with rich symbols and parables that send us on a spiritual treasure hunt for answers can turn up revelations that convince us only God could be speaking. These dreams can confirm messages He's spoken in a still, small voice during our waking hours.

A third reason I believe God speaks to us in dreams is to redeem the time. Why go eight hours a day without communicating with the ones He loves? Similarly, if we are in a season of hurried business and are neglecting to spend as much time with Him as we should, God in His great love for us may choose to speak to us while we are asleep since we are too distracted to sit still long enough for Him to share the deep secrets of His heart.

What the Bible Says About Sleep

God never sleeps or slumbers (Ps. 121:4), and He offers many words of warning in Scripture about the lazy ones who love sleep. But clearly our bodies demand sleep. We know at times God puts His people into a deep sleep—or put the enemy into a deep sleep to help His people (Gen. 2:21, 15:12; Ps. 76:5–6). According to the National Sleep Foundation (NSF), the average adult needs between seven and nine hours of sleep every night. The NSF reports:

> Sleep is an active period in which a lot of important processing, restoration, and strengthening occurs. Exactly how this happens and why our bodies are programmed for such a long period of slumber is still somewhat of a mystery. But scientists do understand some of sleep's critical functions, and the reasons we need it for optimal health and wellbeing.
>
> One of the vital roles of sleep is to help us solidify and consolidate memories. As we go about our day, our brains take in an incredible amount of information. Rather than being directly logged and recorded, however, these facts and experiences first need to be processed and stored; and many of these steps happen while we sleep. . . . Our bodies all require long periods of sleep in order to restore and rejuvenate, to grow muscle, repair tissue, and synthesize hormones.[4]

Of course the scientists left out how God speaks to us in our sleep, but the Bible has plenty to say about sleeping. God intends our sleep to be peaceful (Ps. 4:8, 127:2; Prov. 3:24). I believe part of the reason is so that we can receive more freely from Him in our dreams. Think about it for a minute. God can certainly give a dream to a worried soul, but how much easier is it for us to receive, interpret, and apply what He's showing us when we are at peace? It's the same in our waking hours. It can be more difficult to hear God's still, small voice when our souls are in turmoil.

By contrast, the enemy wants us sleepless. It's one way of tormenting us because our bodies need sleep to function and, again, God wants to send us messages in our dreams that we can decipher when we are awake. Paul told the church at Corinth he had been "through many sleepless nights" in the context of trials and tribulations (2 Cor. 6:5; 11:27 NASB).

Proverbs 3:24 assures us that when we set our heart to keep God's commandments, we will not be afraid in our sleep. It's possible, then, for fear to attack us in our sleep—even through demonic dreams. Psalm 91 assures us those who trust in the Lord will not be afraid of the terror that flies by night. That indicates it is possible for the enemy to terrorize us in our dreams.

God Speaks to Unbelievers in Dreams

Many unbelievers are having divinely inspired dreams, and many desperately seek the meaning of these mysterious messages. Psychologists, New Age mystics, psychics, and those with pagan beliefs have worked to provide resources based on soulish issues or demonic inspirations. We need more believers who understand the principles of decoding dreams so we can interpret the dreams of lost souls who want a supernatural encounter but don't yet realize what they want is a supernatural God named Jesus.

In the Bible we read about God speaking to unbelievers through dreams many times. Let's look at a few of the accounts, starting with Abimelech's warning. Genesis 20 gives the account of Abram lying to King Abimelech about his wife Sarai. Abram thought the king would kill him and take his wife, so he told Abimelech Sarai was his sister. Look what happens next in Genesis 20:3–7 NASB:

> But God came to Abimelech in a dream of the night, and said to him, "Behold, you are a dead man because of the woman whom you have taken, for she is married." Now Abimelech had not come near her; and he said, "Lord, will You slay a nation, even though blameless? Did he not himself say to me, 'She is my sister'? And she herself said, 'He is my brother.' In the integrity of my heart and the innocence of my hands I have done this." Then God said to him in the dream, "Yes, I know that in the integrity of your heart you have done this, and I also kept you from sinning against Me; therefore I did not let you touch her. Now therefore, restore the man's wife, for he is a prophet, and he will pray for you and you will live. But if you do not restore her, know that you shall surely die, you and all who are yours."

Abimelech obeyed the Lord's advice in the dream and saved his life.

In Genesis 40, we read about Pharaoh's chief cupbearer and chief baker each receiving dreams. Pharaoh was mad at his servants and threw them in jail. Both men told Joseph about dreams they had one night. The cupbearer dreamed of a vine with three branches that were blossoming with ripe grapes. He squeezed the grapes and served Pharaoh a cup. Joseph prophesied out of that dream that the three vines represented three days until Pharaoh restored him to his position.

The baker told Joseph about his dream of three baskets of

white bread on his head, with the top basket holding baked foods for Pharaoh. Birds were eating from the basket on his head. Joseph prophesied that the three baskets represented three days and on the third day Pharaoh would behead him, hang him on a tree, and the birds would eat his flesh. Both interpretations were spot on. The dreams unfolded just as Joseph said they would.

Pharaoh, an unbeliever, had two prophetic dreams (Gen. 41). In the first dream, seven healthy cows followed by seven ugly, skinny cows came out of the river. In the second dream, seven heads of plump grain came up, followed by seven thin heads damaged by the wind. These dreams troubled Pharaoh and he sent for the magicians to interpret them. When they could not decipher the meaning, Joseph was summoned. He told Pharaoh the dreams revealed seven years of plenty and seven years of famine.

Daniel 2 chronicles another unbeliever's (Nebuchadnezzar) first dream. The king dreamed of an image with a gold head, silver chest and arms, a bronze belly, legs of iron, and feet that were part iron and clay. Daniel went on to interpret the dream. Nebuchadnezzar had another prophetic dream Daniel interpreted later.

In the New Testament, we also see God giving unbelievers dreams—and quite significant ones. The best example is Pontius Pilate's wife. The Pharisees brought Jesus before Pontius Pilate with one demand: "Crucify Him!" But the Roman ruler's wife delivered a prophetic message to him: "While he was sitting on the judgment seat, his wife sent to him, saying, 'Have nothing to do with that just Man, for I have suffered many things today in a dream because of Him'" (Matt. 27:19 NASB).

We don't know exactly what Pontius Pilate's wife dreamed, but *Benson's Commentary* offers this insight:

Whether she dreamed of the cruel usage of an innocent person, or of the judgments that were about to fall upon those that had any hand in his death, or both, her dream, it seems, was very frightful and distressing, and made such an impression on her mind, that she could not be easy till she had sent an account of it to her husband, who was sitting on the tribunal in the pavement. And the special providence of God must be acknowledged in sending this remarkable dream at this time; for it is not likely that she had heard anything before concerning Christ, at least not so as to occasion her dreaming of him, but that the dream was immediately from God.[5]

Setting the Stage for God Dreams

You can't force your way into the dream world any more than you can force upon yourself the gift of prophecy. But you can set the stage by inviting God into your dream life. As everything else with God, it starts with prayer. If you want to experience God communicating to you through your dreams, *pray and ask Him to give you dreams*. Yes, it can be that easy.

Of course, it's up to the Lord if He chooses to communicate with you in this mode. God communicates in many ways—through a still, small voice; through faint impressions, such as an inner witness; through nature; through other people; and through visions and trances. But if you picked up this book, it's clear you have a hunger to learn about the dream world.

Could it be possible God is waiting on you to get curious enough to ask Him to bring you into the world of prophetic dreams? James 4:2–3 explains that often we *have not* because we *ask not.* If you are asking with pure motives—a hungry heart and a desire to learn and grow—there's no reason not to expect God to open up your dream life. *Expect to have dreams.*

The Bible teaches us that our expectation will not be cut off (Prov. 23:18). When you expect something, you're more likely to receive it. If you don't expect something, you are likely to miss it. There have been times I didn't know a FedEx package was coming to my condo; therefore I left my house to do errands, only to come back to a note on my door saying I'd missed a delivery. I missed it because I wasn't expecting it. If I had expected it, I would have stayed home and waited for it.

Here's another practical example: If your pastor or a friend excitedly tells you the Lord showed them something about your future and promises to call you sometime after dinner to share what they saw or heard, you will wait expectantly. You aren't going to leave your smartphone in another room on vibrate. You aren't going to let your battery drain to zero so that your phone shuts down. You aren't going to take another long phone call and risk missing an incoming call. No, you are going to set that phone right next to you or carry it in your pocket. You are going to make sure the ringer is on. You are going to stay off your phone and wait.

If you ask God to expand your dream life, expect Him to answer. He may not give you a dream the first night. You may have to ask more than once. And it's possible that you are doing something to hinder receiving or remembering your dreams. We'll talk more about remembering dreams later. Right now, let's stay focused on receiving. As I said, it's possible you are doing something to hinder receiving dream communications from God.

Doubt and unbelief are two primary culprits that block any blessing from God. If you doubt God can speak to you in your dreams—or if you don't believe He can—then He probably won't even try. God wants to get His messages across to you. If you have dreams and refuse to believe they are from God—or even doubt they are—you are not likely to give them much credence. You are not likely to apply the truth or take the message to heart. Because He loves you so much, He'll speak to you in a way that you can receive them.

Begin to confess that you are an avid dreamer of God-given dreams. Many times, people who don't have or remember their dreams think that nothing will ever be different for them. Doubt and unbelief block the divine flow. If you discover doubt and unbelief in your heart, repent and ask God to speak to you in your dreams again. Meditate on God's promises about dreams in the Bible, such as Acts 2:17–18, cited earlier in this chapter. Build your faith to dream by speaking the Word of God.

Fear is a huge dream-life killer. It could be possible when you were a child—or even as an adult—the enemy terrorized you in your dreams. You may or may not remember asking God to shut down your dream life. You may or may not even remember the nightmares. The more I teach about dreams, the more I find people who have shut down a true gift of God because they are afraid of what they were seeing or are afraid of missing God by misunderstanding the dream. Fear, in any form, is a dream killer. If you asked God to shut down your dream life, repent.

> Fear, in any form, is a dream killer.

As you settle down to go to sleep, think about God. When David was in the wilderness of Judah, he wrote these words,

When I remember You on my bed, I meditate on You in the night watches. For You have been my help, and in the shadow of Your wings I sing for joy. (Ps. 63:6–7 NASB)

Thinking about God pushes out cares of this world and other thoughts that could keep you up at night, or cause restless sleep. You can also go to sleep listening to instrumental worship music or an audio Bible to create an atmosphere for sweet sleep.

Here's a prayer to help activate your dream life:

Father,

In the name of Jesus, I repent for any doubt, unbelief, or fear I've allowed to creep into my heart knowingly or unknowingly. You are the giver and interpreter of dreams, and I want to see and hear what You are saying to my heart in the night hours. I don't want to miss any opportunity to hear Your voice. Please, open up my dream life so that I can receive fully and understand the messages that are on Your heart for me. Give me dreams to guide me, warn me, and encourage me. Show me things to come, and otherwise share Your will with me.

In Jesus' name, amen.

Chapter 2

THE BIBLICAL
WORLD OF DREAMS

D o you speak dream language? Are you fluent? There's a spiritual vocabulary around dreams, and understanding distinctions is vital to decoding your dream life. You can find this dream language—and its particular vocabulary—in the Bible. Indeed, it's paramount to understand what the Bible says about the dream world so you can avoid New Age pitfalls and get on the same page with God about what He's saying to you in the supernatural realm.

God's supernatural communications are rich with nuances. As I've said, He speaks in a still, small voice, through nature, through impressions, through other people—and in pictures.

In this chapter, we'll focus on God's visual modes of communication. You'll discover answers to questions like:

What is the difference between a dream and a vision? How about an open vision? A night vision? A trance?

What is a lying dream?

How does the dream world intersect with angels and the
supernatural?

What does the Bible say about nightmares?

What does the Bible say about dream interpretation?

We'll explore the Bible's vocabulary around visual communications to lay a strong foundation of truth for decoding your
dreams. This foundation will serve you well as the Word of God
is the bedrock of your faith—and the Word and the Spirit agree
(1 John 5:8).

What the Bible Says About Dreams

The Bible sheds plenty of light on dreams. Before we start diving
into interpretation, wisdom dictates defining dreams according to
Scripture. As we explore biblical dreams, keep in mind God started
talking to people in dreams in the book of Genesis and continued communicating all the way through the book of Revelation.
This proves God has throughout history sent messages through the
dream realm—and He hasn't stopped.

The first time the word *dream* is mentioned in the Bible is in
Genesis 20:3. God came to Abimelech in a dream with a warning.
The Hebrew word for *dream* in that verse is *chalowm*. It can either
refer to an ordinary dream or a dream with a prophetic meaning,
according to *The KJV Old Testament Hebrew Lexicon. Chalowm* is
used sixty-five times in the King James Version of the Bible.

Moving into the New Testament, the Greek word for *dream* is
onar. The word appears in the first chapter of the first book in the

New Testament. In Matthew 1:20, an angel of the Lord appeared to Joseph in a dream, giving him assurance that it was acceptable to take Mary, who was pregnant with Jesus, as his wife. The word *onar* in that verse simply means "dream," according to *The KJV New Testament Greek Lexicon.*

Clearly, not all dreams are from God. But God spoke through dreams repeatedly in both the Old and New Testaments. Sometimes He gave dreams of warning, at other times dreams of instruction, and still other times prophetic dreams.

As you seek to understand the world of dreams, reading through the dreams and their interpretations in the Bible is a strategic way of honing your dream interpretation skill in your life. In other words, pursue a knowledge of biblical dreams as a doorway to open up your understanding of your own dreams. God is a rewarder of those who diligently seek Him (Heb. 11:6). Likewise, when you seek the Word, you are seeking His truth and His way. You are seeking Him. Seek biblical knowledge about dreams and you will find it.

The Difference Between Dreams, Visions, and Trances

This book is all about decoding your dreams—but it's important to understand the different modes of supernatural communication in this realm, including visions and trances, in the context of dreams. Perhaps the most obvious difference between a dream and a vision is that dreams occur while you are asleep, and visions occur while you are awake. Trances, too, occur while you are awake. But let's take a closer look.

What is a vision? The Hebrew word for vision is *chazah*, which means, according to *Strong's Concordance*, "vision, a sight (mentally), i.e., a dream, revelation, or oracle—vision." *Brown-Driver-Briggs* breaks it down as a "vision, as seen in an ecstatic state"; "vision, in the night"; and "divine communication in a vision, oracle, prophecy."

The Greek word for vision is *horasis*, which means, according to the *NAS Exhaustive Concordance*, "the act of seeing, a vision, appearance." *Thayer's Greek Lexicon* defines vision as "the act of seeing, the sense of sight, appearance, visible form, a vision, i.e., an appearance divinely granted in an ecstasy." And *Strong's Exhaustive Concordance* defines vision as "the act of gazing, i.e., (externally) an aspect or (internally) an inspired appearance—a sight, vision."

Again, you dream while you are asleep. You have visions when you are awake. Of course, you can have a vision within a dream, but ultimately a vision within a dream is still part of the dream realm.

Visions

The Bible offers accounts of massively dramatic visions. It's important to note that dramatic visions did not end with the Bible. Rick Joyner has had some dramatic visions that he published in books. His book *Final Quest* describes his panoramic vision of the ultimate quest—the last battle between light and darkness. The late David Wilkerson had a prophetic vision about doomsday that has gone around the world. You can read about it in *The Vision: A Terrifying Prophecy of Doomsday That Is Starting to Happen Now!* We cannot seek out such visions, but we should be open to receiving and recording them.

You can read and study dramatic visions recorded in Scripture. Zechariah's night visions run from Zechariah 1:8 to 6:15. One of Daniel's apocalyptic visions is recorded in Daniel 10:4–9. In fact, Daniel is often called a book of visions because of the many visions the Lord gave him. Visions did not stop in the Old Testament. We read in the New Testament that Ananaias, Paul, Peter, and Cornelius had prophetic visions. The book of Revelation is a dramatic vision of the end-times.

There are categories of visions just as there are categories of dreams. There are three overarching types of prophetic visions: pictures, trances, and open visions.

Pictures: In prophetic circles, you may hear people say they are seeing a picture. These are visual impressions or images that often arise when praying over someone or even in your own private prayer time. When the Holy Spirit shows you a visual, it may be just a flash picture in your mind's eye.

Trances: I've never been in a trance but I know people who have—and it's totally biblical. We only see people falling into a trance a few times in the Bible, but there is enough evidence from the Word of God and from modern expressions to back up this scriptural supernatural experience.

A trance is the state of one who is "out of himself," according to *Easton's Bible Dictionary*. The word *trance* comes from the Greek word *ekstasis*, from which the word *ecstasy* is derived. Peter fell into a trance that opened his eyes to preach the gospel to the Gentiles (Acts 10:10). Paul fell into a trance in which the Lord gave Him a warning and a commission to preach the gospel to the Gentiles (Acts 22:17). I suppose it's hard to describe it if you've not experienced it, but *Smith's Bible Dictionary* goes a little deeper, saying a trance is:

The state in which a man has passed out of the usual order of his life, beyond the usual limits of consciousness and volition, being rapt in causes of this state are to be traced commonly to strong religious impressions. Whatever explanation may be given of it, it is true of many, if not of most, of those who have left the stamp of their own character on the religious history of mankind, that they have been liable to pass at times into this abnormal state.[6]

There are accounts of the late healing evangelist Maria Woodworth-Etter falling into a trance at a St. Louis meeting and standing like a statue for three whole days as attendees of the World Fair looked on in amazement. It's not clear if the trance lasted that long, but she was known to fall into trances that left her frozen for hours at a time—and so did many others who attended her meetings.

"People fell into trances, experienced visions of heaven and hell, collapsed on the floor as if they'd been shot or had died," reports the *Revival Library*. "Thousands were healed of a wide variety of sicknesses and diseases and many believers, even ministers, received mighty baptisms of the Holy Spirit."[7]

Open Visions: Open visions appear to you like a movie or imagery acting out before your eyes. Your eyes are open and you are immune to what is going on around you. It's as if the world around you stops. Paul had an open vision on the road to Damascus (Acts 9:3–9) and also in the night when he received the Macedonian call (Acts 16:9). You can read about one of Ezekiel's dramatic open visions in Ezekiel 1.

Night Visions

There's a debate in the body of Christ over dreams and night visions. Is a dream a vision of the night? Is a night vision a vision you have in the evening hours? Is a night vision something you see when you are in between waking and sleeping states? Is one more symbolic and the other more literal? What is the difference? What does the Bible say? First, let's look at some Scripture references.

God spoke through night visions and visions of the night, terms that seem to be used interchangeably in both the Old and New Testaments. Jacob had visions of the night (Gen. 46:2). Job had a vision of the night (Job 33:15). Daniel had night visions frequently (Dan. 2:19, 7:7, 7:13). Isaiah had a night vision (Isa. 29:7). And Paul had two night visions, or visions of the night (Acts 16:9, 18:9).

We can try to put an end to this debate by looking at the words in these verses and the commentaries. Genesis 46:2–4 NASB: "God spoke to Israel in visions of the night and said, 'Jacob, Jacob!' And he said, 'Here I am.' He said, 'I am God, the God of your father; do not be afraid to go down to Egypt, for I will make you a great nation there. I will go down with you to Egypt, and I will also surely bring you up again; and Joseph will close your eyes.'"

God used the Hebrew word *marah* to describe Jacob's night visions in Genesis. The word means "vision; a mode of revelation."[8] Jacob's visions of the night recorded in Genesis were not dreams. *Gill's Exposition of the Entire Bible* suggests, "And God spake unto Israel in the visions of the night . . . He appeared to Jacob as he lay upon his bed in the night season, and with an articulate voice spoke to him."[9]

Many people lie on their beds without sleeping. If this was a dream, the word *marah*, which means vision, would not have been used in this verse. The Holy Spirit speaks expressly (1 Tim. 4:1).

"In a dream, a vision of the night, when sound sleep falls on men, while they slumber in their beds, then He opens the ears of men, and seals their instruction" (Job 33:15–16 NASB). These verses indicate God can open the ears of men in a dream or a vision of the night. The Hebrew word for *vision* in this verse is *chizzayown*. It means "vision; a vision (in the ecstatic state); vision (in the night); vision, oracle, prophecy (divine communication)," according to *The KJV Old Testament Hebrew Lexicon*. There is a clear distinction then between dreams and visions of the night in Scripture.

Isaiah's night vision is described in the same terms as Job's. In Daniel's experiences, the Hebrew words for vision are *chezev*, which the lexicon defines as "vision, appearance." And the word *night* in all these verses simply means the vision came by night. So, is a night vision something you see when you are in between waking and sleeping states? Possibly but not necessarily.

Benson Commentary explains, "Visions differed from dreams herein, that God imparted his mind to men in dreams when asleep, but in visions when they were awake. And these visions were sometimes communicated by day, but most frequently by night, whence we read of visions of the night, as Genesis 46:2; Job 20:8; and Job 33:15."[10]

Nightmares, Night Terrors, and Sleep Paralysis

Nightmares, night terrors, and sleep paralysis are real phenomenon that are worth exploring in the context of the biblical world of dreams. It seems even the secular world makes room for dark forces that inspire horrifying sleep experiences. Let's look first at some definitions.

The Bible promises us sweet sleep (Prov. 3:24), but sometimes we have to contend for that promise against nightmares. *Merriam-Webster* defines *nightmare* as "an evil spirit formerly thought to oppress people during sleep" and "a frightening dream that usually awakens the sleeper." This is beyond a bad dream. You can sleep through a bad dream, even though it's disturbing, but a nightmare is downright scary, and it's often difficult to fall back to sleep.

When my daughter was three years old, she had dreams of lions chasing her. These were nightmares inspired by an evil spirit, as we read in 1 Peter 5:8 KJV: "Be sober, be vigilant; because your adversary the devil, as a roaring lion, walketh about, seeking whom he may devour."

Also keep in mind that what may seem like a nightmare to you could be a prophetic warning from the Lord that disturbs your soul. In the Bible we read about disturbing warning dreams God gave to men. The book of Daniel contains two accounts of what probably felt to King Nebuchadnezzar like a nightmare but was really the Lord speaking through a dream. The Bible says the king was so troubled that he could not sleep (Dan. 2:2). And in Daniel 4, again, the Bible says he couldn't sleep because of troubling dreams. The Daniel 4 dream was a warning from God to the king to humble himself or face severe consequences. He did not heed the dream and wound up losing his mind for a season until he repented.

A night terror is more serious than a nightmare. *Merriam-Webster* defines it as "a sudden awakening in dazed terror that occurs in children during slow-wave sleep, is often preceded by a sudden shrill cry uttered in sleep, and is not remembered when the child awakes." We know by experience that children are not the only ones who suffer night terrors. Night terrors can bring an all-out panic on the dreamer. Scientists say you may not remember a night terror, but when the enemy of your soul is behind the attack, you may remember it vividly. The Bible clearly speaks of the terror of the night (Ps. 91:5). We are not supposed to fear this. Rather, we are to take authority over it, which we will explore later in this chapter.

While sleepwalking can occur during night terrors, sleep paralysis is altogether different. Sleep paralysis is another unwanted nighttime manifestation some suffer from. *Merriam-Webster* defines the condition as "a complete temporary paralysis occurring in connection with sleep and especially upon waking." The medical world acknowledges natural and spiritual implications of sleep paralysis:

> Sleep researchers conclude that, in most cases, sleep paralysis is simply a sign that your body is not moving smoothly through the stages of sleep . . . Over the centuries, symptoms of sleep paralysis have been described in many ways and often attributed to an 'evil' presence: unseen night demons in ancient times, the old hag in Shakespeare's Romeo and Juliet, and alien abductors. Almost every culture throughout history has had stories of shadowy evil creatures that terrify helpless humans at night. People have long sought explanations for this mysterious sleep-time paralysis and the accompanying feelings of terror.[11]

Many Christians offer accounts of dark dreams—dreams in which the enemy is invading their souls with disturbing images or even full-blown spiritual warfare—accompanied by what the medical world calls sleep paralysis. Some report what they best describe as an unseen force holding them down. Those who could speak often could only speak in a whisper. Others report an inability to speak at all. In each case, they broke through this attack by simply praying in the name of Jesus within themselves and were loosed from the sleep paralysis. Of course, not all sleep paralysis is a spiritual attack. As medical research shows, this can be a glitch in your sleep pattern or could be brought on by certain prescription drugs. But make no mistake—the enemy works to paralyze you in your dreams, and this is not God's will.

How should you ultimately deal with nightmares, night terrors, sleep paralysis, and other interruptions by the enemy? *Refuse fear.* God did not give us a spirit of fear (2 Tim. 1:7), and we don't have to receive the vain imaginations that work their way into our sleep lives. Be cautious of what entertainment you view because it can open the door to demonic attack.

Ultimately, the answer is to pray. Psalm 34:4 KJV assures us: "I sought the LORD, and he heard me, and delivered me from all my fears." Bind the enemy from your dream life (Matt. 18:18). Ask the Lord to give you sweet sleep and prophetic dreams. Think about the Lord as you go to sleep at night. Meditate on His goodness.

When Dreams and Angels Collide

We know through Scripture that God Himself can appear in dreams—and so can angels. In the Bible, when you see the term "the angel of the Lord," it is referring to the pre-incarnate Jesus. For example, the angel of the Lord appeared to Solomon in a dream (1 Kings 3:5, 15). The angel of the Lord also appeared to Jacob in a dream (Gen. 28:12–13). God rebuked Laban in a dream over how he was treating Jacob (Gen. 32:14).

The angel Gabriel appeared to Mary while she was wide awake (Luke 1:26–38). Angels also appeared to Joseph four times in his dreams (Matt. 1:18–25). This doesn't mean that every angel you see in a dream or vision is an angel from heaven. The angel could be symbolizing a messenger or could even be an angel of light (2 Cor. 11:14). If the angel is drawing attention to himself and not pointing to God, God didn't send the angel. Likewise, if the dream contradicts Scripture, God didn't send him.

A Biblical View of Dream Interpretation

I'll repeatedly stress in this book that first and foremost we must turn to God for the interpretation of our dreams. I want to drill this truth home with a series of Scriptures to help convince you to look to the Holy Spirit, your Helper, to help you decode your dream life before turning to a dream definition book or even to a trustworthy dream interpreter.

When Joseph encountered the butler and the baker in prison, "they said to him, 'We each have had a dream, and there is no interpreter of it.' So Joseph said to them, 'Do not interpretations belong to God? Tell them to me, please'" (Gen. 40:8 NKJV).

Joseph, who had a gift of interpreting dreams, still pointed the dreamers to God. Again, you should run to God for answers first, but any dream interpreter should also point you to God as the source of the interpretation. We don't want man's opinion about our dreams. We want God's interpretation.

Paul explained, "But as it is written: 'Eye has not seen, nor ear heard, nor have entered into the heart of man the things which God has prepared for those who love Him. But God has revealed them to us through His Spirit. For the Spirit searches all things, yes, the deep things of God'" (1 Cor. 2:9–10 NKJV). God reveals everything to us through His Spirit, including the meanings of our dreams. Paul also wrote: "These things we also speak, not in words which man's wisdom teaches but which the Holy Spirit teaches, comparing spiritual things with spiritual" (1 Cor. 2:13 NKJV).

First and foremost we must turn to God for the interpretation of our dreams.

You'll be tempted in your quest to understand your dreams to search the internet. While it's okay to Google the meaning of names, Scripture references, geographies, and the meanings of words or symbols, I caution you not to Google the actual meaning of your dream. You'll likely land on a New Age website or might even be asked to pay a dream interpretation fee by someone who appears to be a Christian. Again, let me remind you what Joseph said: "Do not interpretations belong to God?" Seek God. The God who gave you the dream will interpret it or send a godly person who can.

Chapter 3

THE SOURCE
OF DREAMS

We all dream every night. You may not remember a single
dream one night and remember several dreams the next
night. You may go through seasons where you remember your
dreams vividly, then remember nothing or next to nothing in the
next season. Rest assured, you are dreaming while your body is
resting.

There are all sorts of conceptions and misconceptions about
dreams. Some say you can't read or tell time while dreaming,
which is nothing more than man's opinion that aims to tie God's
hands in how He can speak to you through dreams. Others say
we only see the faces of people we know in our dreams, but that's
not accurate either. God can show you the face of someone you've
never seen before but might meet in the future.

Here's what we know about dreams scientifically: The average
adult dreams at least four to six times every night, according to the
National Sleep Foundation.[12] If you sleep eight hours a night, you

may spend as long as two solid hours dreaming. Although your body is resting, your mind shows increased brain activity while you dream.

Scientists reveal that dreams are essential to our well-being. In a study, researchers discovered people who were not allowed to dream experienced increased tension, anxiety, depression, difficulty concentrating, lack of coordination, weight gain, and a tendency to hallucinate.[13] Scientists also believe dreaming helps us with memory function and learning.[14] As I said in chapter 1, God created us to dream.

Also drawing from science, we understand there are five stages of sleep. Dreams mainly happen during REM sleep. *Merriam-Webster's* dictionary defines REM sleep as "a state of sleep that recurs cyclically several times during a normal period of sleep and that is characterized especially by increased neuronal activity of the forebrain and midbrain, depressed muscle tone, dreaming, and rapid eye movements—called also paradoxical sleep, rapid eye movement sleep." Obviously, God can give you a dream at any point during your sleep, but it seems more likely that we'll remember our dreams during REM sleep.

Demonic Dreams, Carnal Dreams, and God Dreams

There are many debates in the dream world. Some argue every dream we have is from God. Others say none of them are from God. Still others say some are and some aren't. Clearly, not all dreams are from God, but I am convinced God is speaking to us in our dreams far more than we realize. Consider Job's words: "For God speaks again and again, though people do not recognize it.

He speaks in dreams, in visions of the night, when deep sleep falls on people as they lie in their beds. He whispers in their ears" (Job 33:14–16 NLT). Other translations say "no one perceives it" (NIV), or "yet no one notices" (NASB), or "we don't always recognize his voice" (CEV), or even "no one pays attention to what he says" (GNT).

As I said, I'm convinced we're dreaming far more than we remember—and I'm also convinced God is speaking to us much more than we understand. We may too easily dismiss God-given dreams because we don't understand them. This is a common temptation and a common mistake. We shouldn't take our dreams lightly. God could be working to send us messages, or the enemy could be attacking, or we could discover unresolved issues in our own souls.

When we have a dream, we need to discern where it originated. Just as prophetic words can come from one of three sources—a demon spirit, our spirits, or the Holy Spirit—there are three over-arching sources of dreams: demonic dreams, carnal dreams, and God dreams.

I love the God dreams, which are the focus of most of this book. You typically don't want to spend time deciphering demonic dreams or carnal dreams beyond the surface level, so it's vital you recognize where your dreams originate. We'll explore each category to give you a clear picture of the dream world as it manifests in your life.

Demonic Dreams

Demonic dreams are just that—inspired by demon powers. Demonic dreams are often, but certainly not limited to, night-mares. And it should be noted, not all nightmares are demon inspired. (We discussed nightmares in chapter 2, so we won't review this information again.) Nightmares are the most obvious kind of demonic dreams, but the enemy is sometimes far more subtle.

How else can we discern demonic dreams? Often, but not always, demonic dreams are in black and white. Demonic dreams are typically laced with fear, carry accusations, include images of death and destruction, and always violate the Word either by all-out defying Scripture or twisting it as the Devil did during Jesus' temptation in the wilderness. Remember, Satan is the father of lies (John 8:44). Demonic dreams can also take the form of spiritual warfare dreams. We'll talk more about spiritual warfare dreams later.

Right now, I want to focus on lying dreams. It is an aspect worth exploring because false spirits rise in the last days to counterfeit or lead us astray from what God is saying or doing. For example, the Bible speaks of lying dreams, which is why all dreams must be judged. The enemy can lie to you through your dreams, and people can try to deceive you by sharing false dreams.

Let these Scriptures sober you and open your spiritual eyes to the reality that not all dreams—whether yours or someone else's—come from the Lord. And keep in mind these are just two of more than a dozen warnings: "For the idols speak delusion; the diviners envision lies, and tell false dreams; they comfort in vain. Therefore the people wend their way like sheep; They are in trouble because there is no shepherd" (Zech. 10:2). And: "I have heard what the prophets say who prophesy lies in my name. They say, 'I had a dream, I had a dream!'" (Jer. 23:25 NIV).

If you are chasing idols—success, fame, or anything other than God—the enemy can and will at times interject lying or false dreams that will fortify your deception. These dreams are not laced with fear. Rather, they bolster your idolatry by confirming your innermost desires that did not come from God. Like true prophecy, true dreams point to or glorify God in your life by inspiring you to follow Him—not serve idols.

If you feel you are having demonic dreams, ask the Lord if there is an open door through which the enemy is gaining access to your dream life. You can open a door through the media you consume, how and with whom you spend your time, and by failing to close doors to your past. We talked about how to deal with demonic dreams in chapter 1. Take authority over them.

Carnal Dreams

Carnal dreams often come out of the lusts of the flesh, the lust of the eyes, and the pride of life (1 John 2:16). They puff you up, lead you toward the idolatry in your heart, and promote selfish plans. Jeremiah 29:8–9 speaks of dreamers causing themselves to dream.

Ecclesiastes 5:7 warns, "For in the multitude of dreams and many words there is also vanity. But fear God." Clearly, the preacher was not speaking of divinely suggested dreams but soulish dreams. And Ecclesiastes 5:3 tells us, "a dream comes when there are many cares" (NIV). Other translations say "too much activity gives you restless dreams" (NLT). The Contemporary English Version assures us, "If you keep thinking about something, you will dream about it." The Good News Translation puts it this way: "The more you worry, the more likely you are to have bad dreams." The International Standard Version says, "Too many worries lead to nightmares." You get the idea. This is not a divinely suggested dream or a demon-inspired nightmare about which Solomon was speaking. These are soulish-carnal dreams.

Consider Paul's warning: "Let no one cheat you of your reward, taking delight in false humility and worship of angels, intruding into those things which he has not seen, vainly puffed up by his fleshly mind, and not holding fast to the Head, from whom all the body, nourished and knit together by joints and ligaments, grows with the increase that is from God" (Col. 2:18–19 NKJV). Paul warned that we can be "vainly puffed up by a fleshly mind." The Amplified Classic translation expounds on this: "vainly puffed up by his sensuous notions and inflated by his unspiritual thoughts and fleshly conceit."

Carnal dreams can also be rooted in soulish desires. I can't count the number of people who come to me about marriage proposals in dreams, and they believe a man in their church is going to pop the question any day. Such dreams usually are not from God but rooted in a deep desire to be married. Likewise, many people dream of living in mansions, driving sports cars, winning the lottery, becoming the boss at their company, or some other self-glorifying scene.

Certainly, God can show you that prosperity is coming to you in a dream or that He is setting you up for a promotion, but when a dream is flashy and you are feeling self-satisfied in the dream, it's often from your soul. Remember, divinely suggested dreams glorify God, not you.

You can use James 3:14–17 NKJV to help you discern soulish dreams from demonic or divinely suggested dreams:

> But if you have bitter envy and self-seeking in your hearts, do not boast and lie against the truth. This wisdom does not descend from above, but is earthly, sensual, demonic. For where envy and self-seeking exist, confusion and every evil thing are there. But the wisdom that is from above is first pure, then

peaceable, gentle, willing to yield, full of mercy and good fruits, without partiality and without hypocrisy.

Subconscious Dream Factors

There are subconscious dream factors in the realm of carnal or soulish dreams. You have a conscious mind and a subconscious mind. *Merriam-Webster's* dictionary defines *subconscious* as "existing in the mind but not immediately available to consciousness." The subconscious mind stores memories and life experiences like a computer stores data.

Also like a computer, your subconscious mind is programmed with data. You don't have to think about how to brush your teeth or ride a bicycle or even drive home from work. These tasks that make up everyday life are essentially on autopilot. Have you ever driven all the way home from work with your mind on a problem and don't even remember how you got there? Your subconscious mind was operating on one level while your conscious mind was working on another.

Your subconscious mind is the part of your soul that needs to be renewed. Paul said, "And do not be conformed to this world, but be transformed by the renewing of your mind, that you may prove what is that good and acceptable and perfect will of God" (Rom. 12:2). When our subconscious mind is not renewed, it can stir dreams in our souls that are worldly. It can also bring up images from our past, hurts and wounds, traumas and the like, that stir our emotions. If you are having dreams of your past—people from your past who hurt you or disturbing events from your past—it could be a sign that you need some emotional healing. The good news is that Jesus is the healer. Surrender the pain to Him, and let Him do His work.

Dreams can come from your subconscious mind. You could be thinking so much about a problem in your conscious mind that your subconscious plays it back in your dream. I've had dreams about being late for a plane the night before I planned to leave. My conscious mind was concerned, at some level, about the alarm not going off, based on my past experience with power outages or failed alarms. So my subconscious mind would bring up that concern in my dream. This was not a dream from God showing me I was going to be late or even a dream from the enemy trying to bring fear of missing my flight.

Food and Chemical Dreams

Still other dreams come from foods we eat too late or medicine we take that impact our brain chemistry. You may have heard of "pizza dreams." This is a phrase that means you ate something spicy, sweet, or heavy late at night. The wrong food at the wrong time can affect your sleep cycles and cause strange dreams. Drinking alcohol can also influence your dreams because science has shown alcohol is metabolized in the second half of the night. Alcohol could even cause nightmares.

If you've ever taken nighttime cold medicine, you've probably had some strange dreams. That's because medications—over-the-counter or prescription—can change your body chemistry and interrupt your REM sleep. Mind-altering drugs clearly affect sleep patterns, but so do antidepressants. Anesthetics, antihistamines, and even herbal drugs can influence our sleep patterns. If you have pretty wild dreams, consider what medications you are taking and how they may be influencing your sleep.

Lucid Dreams

Also in the realm of soulish dreams are lucid dreams. A lucid dream is a dream in which you know you are dreaming while you are dreaming. This is a controversial subject in the body of Christ. Some people claim they can actually control the direction of their dreams. If a dream is from God, you can't control it. God is in control of His messages.

God Dreams

Divinely suggested dreams—or God dreams—are the kinds of dreams I like to have! When you have a God dream, it will confirm, strengthen, warn, convict, and otherwise flow in line with the character of God, the ways of God, the mind of God, and the ministry of the Holy Spirit in your life. Divinely suggested dreams can include prophecy and will reveal God's will, even if through parables. Let's dig deeper into these concepts.

Dreams from God always agree with the Spirit. The Bible clearly tells us the water, the blood, and the Spirit agree (1 John 5:8). Since the Holy Spirit inspired Scripture, it's impossible for a divinely inspired dream to violate Scripture. God would not send you messages in a dream to divorce your wife or commit adultery or engage in any other sinful act.

Likewise, dreams from God do not inspire greed or idolatry. They don't inspire fear or confusion because God has not given us a spirit of fear (2 Tim. 1:7). He is not the author of confusion but of peace (1 Cor. 14:33). Judge messages in your dreams the same way you would judge prophecy. I've written the book *Did the Spirit of God Say That? 27 Ways to Judge Prophecy* to help you.

Always remember, God doesn't condemn you, guilt you, or shame you in your dreams. That's the work of the enemy. "There is therefore now no condemnation for those who are in Christ Jesus, who walk not according to the flesh, but according to the Spirit" (Rom. 8:1).

> Dreams from God always agree with the Spirit.

The Holy Spirit convicts (John 16:8). He does not condemn. Jesus did not come to condemn the world but to save it (John 3:17). How much more His beloved children? When I used to struggle with condemnation, the Lord asked me, "Do you know how to tell the difference between My conviction and the enemy's condemnation?" He quickly told me: "It's love." God disciplines those He loves (Heb. 12:6). He may discipline you—correct your mind-set or reveal wrong motives—in your dreams, but He will not condemn you.

You can also discern a God dream from a demonic or carnal dream by the fruit it produces in your life. Consider this Scripture when you are praying through the source of your dreams:

> Now the works of the flesh are revealed, which are these: adultery, sexual immorality, impurity, lewdness, idolatry, sorcery, hatred, strife, jealousy, rage, selfishness, dissensions, heresies, envy, murders, drunkenness, carousing, and the like. I warn you, as I previously warned you, that those who do such things shall not inherit the kingdom of God. But the fruit of the Spirit is love, joy, peace, patience, gentleness, goodness, faith, meekness, and self-control; against such there is no law. (Gal. 5:19–23)

Dreams and messages from God ultimately glorify God in your life. They should inspire you to pursue God's plans and purposes. That could mean preparing for a promotion or interceding about a warning. Decoding the message should reveal a point of action and completing that action should glorify Jesus. "For the testimony of Jesus is the spirit of prophecy" (Rev. 19:10 KJV).

Take the time to discern the source of your dream before acting on it. Ask the Holy Spirit to help you. He will always confirm His own messages.

Chapter 4

DREAM
CLASSIFICATIONS

O ver the years I've had more disturbing dreams than I care
to remember. I still remember recurring dreams that manifested at marked intervals. I rejoice in dreams that pointed me in
a new direction in life, that warned me of danger, and that stirred
me to pray. I cherish all divinely suggested dreams because they are
God's messages communicated in a masterpiece of pictures.

There are many different types of dreams—and a purpose for
each one. Indeed, everything God does has a purpose. He's pur-
poseful in who He talks to, what He says, when He says it, why He
expresses Himself in a dream instead of another communication
mode, where He shares what's on His heart, and how He leads
you into the interpretation. It's hard to classify dreams in a neat
and tidy box, because you can't put God in a box. But if you think
about your dream life, you can identify classifications and patterns
even if you don't fully comprehend the messages.

Understanding dream classifications will help you see the bigger picture God is trying to show you. Beyond the demonic and carnal dreams we spoke of earlier, we'll dive into explanations and examples of different dream categories, from dreams that offer direction, to dreams that offer warnings, to dreams that offer revelation, and to other dream types that will help you decipher what God is saying in your dreams.

Literal or Parabolic-Symbolic

There are two overarching categories of dreams: literal and parabolic-symbolic. What you see in a literal dream may not be something that actually happened or that will happen, but God is showing you through the dream what is taking place without the need for much, if any, interpretation.

With that said, some would argue dreams have no literal visuals—that they are always parabolic and symbolic. I disagree with that argument. I do believe all dreams have symbols, colors, names, and other dream language that must be deciphered to discover deeper layers of meaning. But God communicates some dreams as straightforwardly as He speaks to your heart in the familiar still, small voice. When an angel warned Joseph in a dream, he didn't have to decipher six symbols and two parables to get the message (Matt. 2:3).

Consider some *Merriam-Webster* dictionary definitions of the word *literal*: "free from exaggeration or embellishment" and "characterized by a concern mainly with facts." Literal dreams are marked by reality. The people in the dream are the people the dream concerns. What was said or done in a dream has bearing on what has or will be said and done in reality. God can use literal dreams in any of the categories we'll explore in this chapter.

Let me give you one example of a literal dream I had. A woman I'd known for many years, we'll call her Cindy, who was very hurt and wounded—a woman who carried a spirit of rejection and lived in an abusive environment—created a soul tie with me. We were friends, the relationship became codependent. When I hired new staff in the ministry, I suggested Cindy take a breather from serving and spend some time with the Lord healing, because I knew she was struggling with some personal issues.

Cindy didn't appreciate the gesture. Instead, she became angry and cut off the friendship. A few months later, I had a dream in which she approached me with an angry expression on her face and said, "You slammed the door on me!" The Lord was showing me how she felt. I have no doubt these were the literal thoughts she was thinking and perhaps even words she shared with others. That dream spurred me to continue praying for Cindy's total healing.

Most dreams are indeed parabolic or symbolic in nature. *Parabolic* simply means that it's communicated as a parable, some sort of story that illustrates a principle. This makes sense, given Jesus spoke to the crowds in parables. Like Christ's parables—the parable of the sower (Matt. 13) is a great example—parables are spiritually discerned. They require prayer and searching to understand.

God wants us to search out our dreams and gain spiritual discernment. "It is the glory of God to conceal a matter, but the glory of kings is to search out a matter" (Prov. 25:2 NASB). Parables and symbols, I believe, keep us from depending on our own minds and press us to seek God for the hidden mystery He wants to reveal.

The rest of the chapter is sectioned into short descriptions of different types of dreams. These are addressed in alphabetical order, not in order of prominence or importance.

Calling Dreams

God can reveal your calling—or the next stage of your calling—in a dream. You may not understand what God is saying at the time. We see this type of dream plainly in Joseph's life:

> Now Joseph had a dream, and he told it to his brothers; and they hated him even more. So he said to them, "Please hear this dream which I have dreamed: There we were, binding sheaves in the field. Then behold, my sheaf arose and also stood upright; and indeed your sheaves stood all around and bowed down to my sheaf."
>
> And his brothers said to him, "Shall you indeed reign over us? Or shall you indeed have dominion over us?" So they hated him even more for his dreams and for his words. Then he dreamed still another dream and told it to his brothers, and said, "Look, I have dreamed another dream. And this time, the sun, the moon, and the eleven stars bowed down to me." So he told it to his father and his brothers; and his father rebuked him and said to him, "What is this dream that you have dreamed? Shall your mother and I and your brothers

indeed come to bow down to the earth before you?" (Gen. 37:5–10 NKJV)

Joseph would indeed reign over his brothers and they would bow down to him—but not for a long while. The same way we often do, Joseph went through a process that took him from where he was to the fulfillment of the dream God gave him. His brothers became jealous and angry, threw him into a pit, and sold him as a slave. He wound up in prison before he eventually rose to rule Egypt as Pharaoh's second in command—and rule over his brothers.

Cleansing Dreams

We live in the world, but we are not citizens of the world. This world is not our ultimate home. However, the spirit of the world is lurking everywhere. You can't drive down the highway without seeing a sexually suggestive billboard. You can't go to the gym or a restaurant without hearing music that suggests depression, death, or some other ungodly theme. You can't even watch wholesome TV shows—or sports—without advertisements for alcohol or something else Christians shouldn't have invading their living rooms. Then there are the people you run into at work or on the streets who have foul or perverse spirits.

God can choose to cleanse you from the filth of the world you come in contact with during your everyday life through your dreams. Many times dreams of being in a bathroom or shower are cleansing dreams, even if you didn't come into agreement with the fruitless deeds of darkness (Eph. 5:11).

Conviction Dreams

God can convict you of sin or wrong attitudes in your dreams and visions. When the Lord wanted to correct Peter's bias against the Gentiles, He gave him a vision in a trance:

> [Peter] saw heaven opened and an object like a great sheet bound at the four corners, descending to him and let down to the earth. In it were all kinds of four-footed animals of the earth, wild beasts, creeping things, and birds of the air. And a voice came to him, "Rise, Peter; kill and eat." But Peter said, "Not so, Lord! For I have never eaten anything common or unclean." And a voice spoke to him again the second time, "What God has cleansed you must not call common." This was done three times. And the object was taken up into heaven again. (Acts 10:11–16 NKJV)

Peter responded to the correction and shared the gospel with the Gentiles.

Deliverance Dreams

Jesus came to set the captives free (Luke 4:18). Deliverance ministers cast out demons and break oppression. God can and does set people free in their dreams. If you dream you are breaking free from an addiction or a bondage—or a wrong thought pattern, fear, rejection, and so on—wake up with worship and praise and thank God. You may also dream others are being set free or that you are being used as a deliverance minister. This could signal that the Lord will break bondages over the person or people in your dream or that He is calling you into deliverance ministry.

Direction Dream

God can lead us and guide us—provide us clear direction for life and ministry—through our dreams. Some of those dreams may also fall into the categories of warnings, like the three wise men who followed the star in the east to discover the baby Christ. "Then, being divinely warned in a dream that they should not return to Herod, they departed for their own country another way" (Matt. 2:12 NKJV).

Paul received clear direction in a vision: "And a vision appeared to Paul in the night. A man of Macedonia stood and pleaded with him, saying, 'Come over to Macedonia and help us.' Now after he had seen the vision, immediately we sought to go to Macedonia, concluding that the Lord had called us to preach the gospel to them" (Acts 16:9–10 NKJV).

Divine Connection Dreams

God can pave the way for divine connections through dreams. This has happened to me personally. I once received direction to consult with a man of God whom I encountered in a dream. I did not know this man personally, but I knew of him. I didn't even follow his ministry at the time, and there was no natural urge to work with him or get to know him.

In my dream, I was preparing to step onto a platform from which I'd never ministered. It was a huge platform. I was racing back and forth preparing for the opportunity to minister. This man of God was standing in the background, steadily watching me walk to and fro. After some time, he called me over to him and offered some advice: "I've been where you are going. I know the way. Trust me. Just give them one or two things. That's all they can handle." Then he repeated himself.

We know that just because you see a person in a dream doesn't always mean you will meet that person. A figure in your dream could literally be that person or could be a symbol of what that person represents. In this case, I believe both realities apply. This man represented prayer, intercession, and revival. But I was also to receive advice from him in real life. A friend of mine knew this man of God, so I reluctantly reached out, told my friend the dream, and asked for an opportunity to share it in the context of a prophetic word I received ten years earlier about a Third Great Awakening coming to America.

The man of God agreed to speak with me, and I shared my dream. He asked me to share it a second time. Then he asked where I lived. After I told him, he said, "Maybe we're supposed to do something together in your city." He then asked if I knew one of his friends, a man of God who lived near me. I told him I didn't but immediately reached out to connect with his friend. Within a week I was sitting at lunch with both men. That dream—and following through with the dream—set the stage for many doors to open during that phase of my ministry.

Divine Strategy Dreams

Jacob needed a strategy. He had worked for Laban, his uncle, for fourteen years as a dowry for Laban's two daughters, but Jacob had nothing material to show for it. Laban was a dishonest man who built his riches on Jacob's labor and changed his wages ten times (Gen. 31:7). As Jacob described it: If he said thus: "The speckled shall be your wages," then all the flocks bore speckled. And if he said thus: "The streaked shall be your wages," then all the flocks bore streaked. So God has taken away the livestock of your father and given them to me.

> And it happened, at the time when the flocks conceived, that I lifted my eyes and saw in a dream, and behold, the rams which leaped upon the flocks were streaked, speckled, and gray-spotted. Then the Angel of God spoke to me in a dream, saying, "Jacob." And I said, "Here I am." And He said, "Lift your eyes now and see, all the rams which leap on the flocks are streaked, speckled, and gray-spotted; for I have seen all that Laban is doing to you. I am the God of Bethel, where you anointed the pillar and where you made a vow to Me. Now arise, get out of this land, and return to the land of your family." (Gen. 31:10–13 NKJV)

God gave Jacob a dream that brought justice into his life through a divine strategy. Pay attention to your dreams. God could provide a strategy for your health, your finances, your family, your business, or your ministry.

Epic Dreams

Epic dreams are just that—*epic*. We can understand what an epic dream is by looking at *Merriam-Webster*'s definition of the word *epic*: "a long narrative poem in elevated style recounting the deeds of a legendary or historical hero." Epic dreams and visions are long, vivid, and dramatic. Some in the dream interpretation world call them "cosmic" dreams. These are the kinds of dreams you don't soon forget and can change the course of your life or even how you view God. In Daniel 7, Daniel had an epic dream and night visions of four beasts. In the book of Revelation, John had an epic vision.

Healing Dreams

Healing dreams can bring physical healing to our bodies or emotional healing to our souls—or the promise of healing that builds faith, enabling us to walk through afflictions and trials. You might see someone praying for you or see yourself praying for someone else's healing—even laying hands on them—in a dream. If God can heal us while we are awake, He can certainly heal us while we are asleep. Sometimes with deep, painful emotional issues that we may reject or avoid while we are awake, God deals with them through dreams.

Innovation Dreams

Some call these invention dreams. God can give us creative ideas in our dreams or give us dreams symbolizing new inventions that could even change the world. God's wisdom in a dream can birth witty inventions as Proverbs 8:12 KJV tells us: "I wisdom dwell with prudence, and find out knowledge of witty inventions."

Intercession Dreams

In an intercession dream, you are usually an observer. You may witness something in the dream that presents a need, a concern, or some problem. Maybe in the dream someone you recognize is sick or in danger. On the positive side, in the dream perhaps someone you are familiar with is about to walk into a new opportunity. You'll often wake up with an intercessory prayer burden—an urge to pray that doesn't lift until the Lord has used you to accomplish His will in the matter.

Problem-Solving Dreams

Problem-solving dreams are just what they sound like—dreams that offer revelation about how to solve a problem you're experiencing. This could be a personal problem, a family problem, a business problem—any type of problem. God is the ultimate problem solver.

Prophetic Dreams

Prophetic dreams are predictive in nature. We have a promise that the Holy Spirit will show us things to come (John 16:13). Sometimes He shows us in our dreams. Prophetic dreams offer a glimpse into the future through God's eyes. You may not even understand what you are seeing, and you may at first reject the possibility of it happening. Prophetic dreams could manifest quickly in the natural realm, or it could take many years for them to come to pass. As with any prophetic word, God does His part, but we have to do our part and be open to see how His promises manifest in our reality. Remember though, prophetic dreams require wisdom and discernment to decode their meaning.

Recurring Dreams

Recurring dreams are somewhat repetitive in nature. The definition of *recurring* is "to come again to mind," according to *Merriam-Webster's* dictionary. Just as you can have recurring thoughts—whether good or bad—you can have recurring dreams from the enemy or from God. The dictionary also defines *recurring* as "to occur again after an interval: occur time after time."

At a meeting during which I was teaching on dreams, I had a word of knowledge that someone in the audience was having recurring dreams about dying—they saw themselves die. This was a risky piece of information to receive, because the crowd was lighter during the morning session, and it would take humility for anyone to admit their death vision in their dream life. But a teenage girl lifted her hand, crying, saying she was the one.

I asked her if these recurring death dreams were mirror images of each other. Did she die the same way each time? No, she said, sometimes it was by a car accident and other times falling off a building and still other times getting attacked by an assailant. But she always saw herself die in the dream.

The girl was weeping on her mother's shoulder when the Lord gave me another word of knowledge: someone close to her had died, and she had unforgiveness in her heart as a result. She was simultaneously grieving and walking in unforgiveness; therefore it opened her up to enemy attack in her dreams. This was a tormenting spirit, which the enemy releases on the unforgiving (Matt. 18:34)—even if you are a God-fearing, grieving teenager. I led her into repentance and healing prayers. That slammed the door shut on the enemy.

I've had recurring dreams about pregnancies, which I'll share later. But I've also had recurring dreams about missing planes, which was frustrating. In one dream, I missed a plane to Charlotte, North Carolina. I had a ticket, but I missed the flight. When I did some word studies, I discovered Charlotte means "free." It's also the second-largest financial center in the United States, just steps behind New York's financial district.

In another dream, I was flying out of New York City. My flight was scheduled to leave at 7:30 a.m. It was 7:00 a.m., and I was not yet at the airport. There was no way I could make the flight, but then it was delayed until 9:00 a.m., so I set out to make it. In my dreams, as well as for others, planes can have something to do with ministry. In this season, I was concerned that I was missing opportunities due to a lack of adequate help in the ministry. The Lord was showing me an urgent need to bring more help on board so I didn't miss what He wanted me to do. The delay was Him giving me more time to get things in order due to the rapid growth of the ministry.

Spiritual Warfare Dreams

Spiritual warfare dreams are not necessarily from the enemy. Spiritual warfare dreams can give you a heads-up on what the enemy has planned against you or reveal the enemy's strategy against you or someone else. Spiritual warfare dreams are often quite intense and dramatic.

I had a spiritual warfare dream in which a group of us from my church, Awakening House of Prayer in Fort Lauderdale, were being chased. We were in a tall office building. I cannot remember who all was in the group because we were split up. One of the young women who was with me went into the bathroom, came out, and remarked, "It's not too bad in there."

I then went into the bathroom and found a dead body hunched over the toilet. It looked kind of like the young woman from my group who had come out of the bathroom and made the comment. Suddenly, that dead body disappeared. The toilet seat had urine all over it. I tried to clean it up but it soaked through the paper. The urine just kept coming back no matter how much I tried to clean it up.

What does this mean? Being chased is associated with threats and demand a call to prayer. Urine deals with defiling words or acts or some offense or foul spirit. The toilet deals with cleansing or deliverance. The death in this scene wasn't literal because there was no blood. In dreams, literal deaths tend to include blood. The death was more likely revealing this young woman's need to die to self, but she was resisting God's message.

In the dream, I continued walking with the young woman after the bathroom incident. This young woman was a prophetic intercessor and prayer warrior in her own right but had serious hurts, wounds, and pride issues, as well as unforgiveness. The Lord was showing me she was not ready to deal with the level of spiritual warfare in the ministry until she was healed. And her unwillingness to confront issues in her heart were sidelining her. Still, the Lord wanted me to disciple and walk with her through the process.

Strengthening Dreams

God can use dreams to strengthen your resolve and build your faith. We read about God doing this for Gideon, who took quite a lot of convincing in the first place that God wanted to use him:

> And when Gideon had come, there was a man telling a dream to his companion. He said, "I have had a dream: To my surprise, a loaf of barley bread tumbled into the camp of Midian; it came to a tent and struck it so that it fell and overturned, and the tent collapsed." Then his companion answered and said, "This is nothing else but the sword of Gideon the son of Joash, a man of Israel! Into his hand God has delivered Midian and the whole camp." And so it was, when Gideon heard the telling of the dream and its interpretation, that he worshiped. He returned to the camp of Israel, and said, "Arise, for the Lord has delivered the camp of Midian into your hand." (Judges 7:13–15 NKJV)

Keep in mind this wasn't even Gideon's own dream. See how the dreams other people have and share with us—whether directly about us or not—can build our faith and give us confidence to move forward? Don't hesitate to share a dream with someone if the Lord leads you to share. By the same token, don't be too quick to share any and every dream you have. We'll talk more about that in a later chapter.

Valley of Decision Dreams

"Trust in the LORD with all your heart, and lean not on your own understanding; In all your ways acknowledge Him, and He shall direct your paths" (Prov. 3:5–6). Sometimes our souls are conflicted or confused about a big decision. Sometimes we reason ourselves out of God's prophetic wisdom because we have our eyes on natural circumstances. God may choose to surpass your weary soul and speak straight to you while your eyes are closed and your mind is resting—He may choose to speak to your spirit through a dream that helps you settle into peace on your best course of action.

Warning Dreams

God can send us clear warnings in dreams. In fact, many of the dreams recorded in the Bible are warning dreams. Abimelech was warned in a dream not to touch Abraham's wife (Gen. 20). Laban was warned in a dream not to bless or curse Jacob on his way home (Gen. 31:24). Pharaoh was warned in a dream about seven years of famine (Gen. 41). The Magis were warned in a dream not to go back to Herod after visiting Bethlehem and seeing the baby Christ (Matt. 2:12). And an angel warned Joseph in a dream to get to Egypt before Herod executed every male baby in Bethlehem (Matt. 2).

Word of Knowledge Dreams

God can give you a word of knowledge in your dreams. A word of knowledge is a revelation that offers information related to either the past or the present. God may show you a mentor or a stranger in your dream that offers you a word of knowledge that helps you deal with a problem or issue at hand.

Chapter 5

SCRIPTURAL
DREAM CODES

Have you ever looked up the meaning of your name? I had dinner with a name etymology expert in Ireland, and he rattled off root meanings of names—some of them rather surprising. It was fascinating. As it turns out, many of those online dictionaries offering the meanings of names are wrong. That's why I don't advocate putting a lot of stock in name and dream dictionaries online.

When God created Adam, one of his first assignments was to name the animals. Names are important to God. In Jewish culture, baby names hold intense significance. The Jewish people know every time they call their child's name they are prophesying his or her future. When God changed Abram's name to Abraham, it was telling. Abraham means "father of many nations." When Abraham heard his name called, he heard "father of many nations," which built his faith to stand on the promise of God for his life.

The many names of God are significant. *Jehovah Nissi*, for

example, means the Lord My Banner. *Jehovah Rapha* means the Lord that Heals. *Jehovah Jireh* means the Lord Will Provide. And *Jehovah Shalom* means the Lord Is Peace. Beyond Abraham, the names of Bible personalities often have deep meaning, so if you dream of someone named Joshua in a dream, you should look up the biblical meaning of the name.

The same principle holds true for places. There are many places mentioned in the Bible, from Jezreel to Jerusalem and from Bethel to Bethlehem. All these places have names with significant meanings that can inform what God is saying to you in a dream.

Although your dream life is in many ways subjective to your worldview and your experience with God, there are dream codes in the Bible that serve as a foundation for all interpretation. The responsible dream interpreter starts with the Word of God in all interpretation—unless the Spirit of God directs in another way.

Keep in mind that since dreams can have layers of meaning, it's possible a symbol could have scriptural ties and subjective ties. We want to explore all facets of our dreams and stay prayerful along this prophetic treasure hunt, searching out what God is really saying.

Scriptural dream codes include names, places, colors, numbers, and symbols. We'll explore those in the pages ahead, which will reveal the complex world of dream meanings and maybe answer a few questions you've had about your own dreams.

Biblical Names and Places

You can study names found in the pages of the Bible using a free online resource called *Hitchcock's Bible Names*. Published in the

1800s, it contains more than twenty-five hundred Bible and Bible-related proper names and their meanings. You can Google the dictionary for a safe resource on Bible names.

Let's say you have a dream about someone named Aaron. You could look up the name and find out it means "a teacher; lofty; mountain of strength." That could speak into the overarching meaning of the dream. Joel means "he who wills or commands." That could give you a clue about what the Lord is saying, depending on what Joel said or did in the dream. Peter means "a rock or stone." So if you dream of someone named Peter giving you a gift, it could mean someone solid is going to mentor you. Of course, it could mean many things based on the context and other symbols and story lines.

While exploring what God is saying through names in your dreams, you can also look at what these Bible characters stood for in Scripture. Aaron was Moses' prophet. Peter was a strong-willed man of revelation. As you can see, interpreting dreams is complex and requires prayer and insight from the Holy Spirit. Dream interpretation is often like a treasure hunt. It takes some time, but when you strike gold you've tapped into true riches that make it all worthwhile.

Regarding places in the Bible, the Lord gave me a prophetic word some years ago that said it was time for the church to return to Antioch. That could just as well have been a dream. The principle is the same. What did the Lord mean by this? I looked up Antioch in my Bible concordance. When I read Acts 14, prophetic revelation for the body of Christ—particularly the leadership of the body of Christ—began to unfold: When Paul and Barnabas were serving together in the mission fields, they made a return visit to Lystra, Iconium, and Antioch. With the return to Antioch, they had a clear mandate: to "[strengthen] the souls of the disciples, exhorting them to continue in the faith, and saying, 'We must through many tribulations enter the kingdom of God' " (Acts 14:22).

As I meditated on this verse, it became abundantly apparent how different the apostles' message was from what we hear in most local churches—and on most Christian TV channels—today. The apostles understood that we are in a spiritual war against principalities, against powers, against the rulers of the darkness of this age, against spiritual hosts of wickedness in the heavenly places (Eph. 6:12). The apostle urged and warned believers to fight the good fight of faith and made it clear that it wouldn't be easy.

The prophetic takeaway: We need to "return to Antioch." We need to return to sound doctrine that strengthens the spirits and souls of the disciples, encourages them to contend for the true faith, and refuses to sugarcoat the Christian walk. We need to "return to Antioch" and leave behind the Hollywood Christianity, the pillow prophets, the prosperity gospel, and the other foolish practices that have crept into the twenty-first-century church while we were sleeping. We need to "return to Antioch" and walk with Christ no matter what it costs us. We need to be found faithful when the Lord returns.

I'll give you one more example. This can be applied to any biblical city that appears in your dream. Let's say you have a dream you are in Bethlehem. With Bethlehem or any city, you should always go to the first reference of the name to start your interpretive journey. In hermeneutics—which deals with interpreting Bible texts—this is called the law of first mention. The law of first mention demands we go to the first mention of a person, place, or thing—or doctrine—to get a foundational understanding of its meaning.

Bethlehem was first mentioned in Genesis 48:7 in the context of Jacob burying his wife Rachel. Next, Bethlehem is mentioned as the city to which Ruth and Naomi returned after death hit their family. Ruth gleaned grain for provision in Bethlehem. Bethlehem was also King David's birthplace and the place he was anointed (1 Sam. 16:4–13). Three of David's warriors put their lives at risk in Bethlehem to bring him water from a well while he was on the run from Saul. Of course, Christ was also born in Bethlehem, and King Herod ordered the slaughter of many children there. Modern-day Bethlehem is about five miles south of Jerusalem, the capital city of Israel.

If you have a dream involving Bethlehem, what is God saying? This is where context matters. Names matter, colors matter, symbols matter, but context—the setting, environment, or conditions—help inform the meaning.

What was happening to you in Bethlehem? What were your emotions? Generally, dreams of Bethlehem are good. Bethlehem means "house of bread." But are you at war in Bethlehem? Is there a struggle? This could mean struggle over provision (natural bread). It could be a struggle over revelation (spiritual bread as explained in Matthew 4:4). It could mean a struggle over deliverance, which Jesus called the children's bread (Matt. 15:26). Understanding context and understanding the broader base of Scripture helps inform your dreams.

Colors

What do colors mean in your dreams? First, we must examine what colors mean in the Bible. While colors have different meanings in various cultures, I believe it's essential to understand what the Bible says first. God is a colorful God. His creation is full of beautiful colors—and so is heaven. The rainbow He displays as a sign of His covenant with man never to flood the earth again is very colorful (Gen. 9:13).

The King James Version lists fifteen colors: bay, black, blue, brown, crimson, green, grey, hoar, purple, red, scarlet, sorrel, vermillion, white, and yellow (also used to describe gold). We won't go through all of them here, but I want to give you a glimpse of the common Bible colors that may appear in your dreams.

Black

Black typically relates to sin (Job 6:15–16), sickness and disease (Job 30:30), death (Jude 1:12–13), sorrow and mourning (Jer. 8:21; Gen. 37:34; Isa. 50:3; Rev. 6:12), and famine (Lam. 4:8, 5:10; Rev. 6:5–6).

Three times in Scripture, however, it offers the meaning of health or beauty (Lev. 13:37; Song 1:5–6, 5:11). It can also speak about judgment (Lev. 13:37; Job 3:5; Jer. 13:37).

Blue

Blue can symbolize heaven (Ezek. 1:26, 24:10, 25:4).

Many curtains and coverings in the Bible are blue, including holy coverings and royal apparel in Exodus 28:31, Esther 8:15, and Numbers 4:5–7.

Blue in the Bible also deals with chastening (Prov. 20:30 KJV).

On the negative side, blue can symbolize idolatry and spiritual adultery (Jer. 10:8–9; Ezek. 23:3–8).

Green

Green speaks of life, growth, rest, and good fruit. Consider that green vegetation is healthy whereas brown plants lack water or nutrients. We read: "The Lord called your name, Green Olive Tree, Lovely and of Good Fruit" (Jer. 11:16 NKJV). And again: "For he shall be like a tree planted by the waters, which spreads out its roots by the river, and will not fear when heat comes; But its leaf will be green, and will not be anxious in the year of drought, nor will cease from yielding fruit" (Jer. 17:8 NKJV).

Other Scriptures that demonstrate the biblical meaning of green on the positive side include Hosea 14:8, Psalm 23:2–3, and Psalm 52:8.

On the negative side, green can be associated with plague or death (Lev. 13:49, 14:37) or cutting down (Ps. 37:2).

Purple

Purple is a color of royalty in the Bible (Ex. 27:16; Prov. 32:22; Jer. 10:9; Song 7:5; Acts 16:14; Luke 16:19). Purple dye was expensive in Bible times and was usually worn by the wealthy or kings (Judg. 8:26).

Purple, then, symbolizes prosperity (Ex. 28:5; Ezek. 27:7).

On the negative side, it can also speak of the corruption of wealth (Rev. 17:4).

Red

Red often symbolizes the blood of Jesus (Rev. 1:5; 1 Peter 1:18–19; Col. 1:20–21).

In the Bible, we find red also associated with the sky as a sign of the times (Matt. 16:2–3); the great dragon (Rev. 12:3); plagues (Lev. 13:19); wine (Prov. 23:31); horses (Zech. 1:8); skin color of Esau (Gen. 25:25); or stew (Gen. 25:30).

Look at the context of the color red in these verses for deeper meaning, especially if you dreamed, for example, of red stew.

Red can be a symbol of war (Nah. 2:3; 2 Kings 3:22), speak of the temptation to sin (Gen. 25:30; Prov. 23:31), or mark vengeance (Isa. 63).

White

White can stand for righteousness and cleansing from unrighteousness (Ps. 51:7; Rev. 6:11, 7:13–14). "Though your sins are like scarlet, they shall be as white as snow; though they are red as crimson, they shall be like wool" (Isa. 1:18 NIV).

But white in the Bible is also associated with teeth (Gen. 49:12); the milk of the Word (1 Cor. 3:1–2); manna from heaven in the wilderness (Ex. 16:31); baskets for food (Gen. 40:17; Jer. 24:2); hair (Matt. 5:36; Rev. 1:14); fields that are ready for harvest (John 4:35); and end-times symbols such as stones (Rev. 2:17), clouds (Rev. 14:14), and thrones (see Rev. 20:11).

On the negative side, white can point to a false righteousness (Matt. 23:27; Acts 23:3), leprosy, or plague (Lev. 13:4; Num. 12:10; 2 Kings 5:27).

Yellow (gold)

Gold represents the glory of God (Rev. 3:18) on the positive side, as well as wealth (Ezek. 7:19).

It represents leprosy (disease) on the negative side (Lev. 13).

Bible Numbers

Numerology, the study of numbers, can and does get off base in a hurry. We must avoid the New Age concept of numerology like the plague. But biblical numerology is, well, biblical. It should seem obvious to any serious Bible student that God is a God of numbers, though some still debate it. Numbers often have both a theological and symbolic meaning in Scripture, and the numbers we see in dreams could reveal what God is saying or planning to do in our lives or in the world. Numbers can also have more than one meaning in Scripture.

The goal of this section is not to offer you a complex study of numerology. Indeed, entire books have been written on the topic. My goal is to give you a primer on biblical numerology so you can see how God can and does speak through numbers in dreams.

One

The number one means God or unity. "Hear, O Israel: The LORD our God, the LORD is one!" (Deut. 6:4 NIV). In marriage, the two become one (Matt. 19:6). Jesus prayed that we would all be one as the Father and Son are one (John 17:21).

Two

The number two can speak to unity on the positive side and division or double-mindedness on the negative side. Jesus sent out disciples two by two (Mark 6:7). God told Noah to bring two of each animal onto the ark (Gen. 1:27; 2:20, 24). Elijah asked the Israelites how long they would waver between two opinions regarding whom they would serve (1 Kings 18:21). Jesus speaks of a choice of entering the narrow gate that leads to life or the broad gate that leads to destruction (Matt. 7:13–14).

The number two can also speak to establishing a truth (Deut. 17:6; Gen. 41:32) or dual rulership (Dan. 8:20–21; Rev. 13:11).

Three

The number three typically represents the Godhead—Father, Son, and Holy Spirit (Matt. 28:19; John 14:26; 1 Peter 1:2).

You can also draw lines between the number three and wondrous works of God. God gave Moses the Law on day three (Ex. 9:11). Jonah was delivered from the belly of a whale after three days (Jonah 1:17). Christ was raised from the dead on the third day (Matt. 12:40).

Four

The number four points to completion in many Scriptures, as well as God's creative works.

There are four corners of the earth (Rev. 7:1), four rivers coming from the garden of Eden (Gen. 2:10), and four winds that blow (Dan. 7:2). We have four seasons.

There are four creatures in Revelation 4. Four is a number found repeatedly in Scripture relating to the end times (Zech. 1:18–21; Zech. 6:1–8; Rev. 9:13–14).

Five

The number five represents grace and redemption.

In the Mosaic law, five types of animals were sacrificed.

There were five porches at the pool of Bethesda where Jesus healed the lame man (John 5:1–9).

Six

Six is the number of man. Man was created on the sixth day (Gen. 1:24–31). Man works six days and rests one (Ex. 31:15; 20:9).

Six in the Bible is sometimes linked with God's enemies (Dan. 3:1; Rev. 13:18; 1 Chron. 20:6).

Seven

Seven is found in Scripture representing perfection, wholeness, or completeness. After God created the earth in six days, He rested on the seventh day and called it the Sabbath (Gen. 2:1–3).

The Israelites marched around Jericho for seven days and seven times on the seventh day to bring about victory (Josh. 6:15).

Jesus told Peter to forgive seventy times seven times, which suggests limitless forgiveness (Matt. 18:21–22).

Eight

Eight in Scripture represents new beginnings.

Eight people found salvation on Noah's ark when God flooded the earth (Gen. 7:13). God started new with those people after the flood.

David was number eight among his brothers and marked a new beginning for Israel after Saul's foul kingship (1 Sam. 16:10–13).

Nine

Nine can represent the Holy Spirit or judgment.

There are nine gifts of the Holy Spirit (Gal. 5:22–23).

There are also nine fruits of the Holy Spirit (1 Cor. 12:7–10).

On the judgment side, we see the Holy Spirit convicts the world of judgment (John 16:7–11).

Ten

The number ten is a multiple of five, so many see it as double grace.

Twelve

Twelve largely represents government in Scripture.

We see there are twelve tribes of Israel.

There are twenty-four elders (twelve times two) around the throne of God.

There are twelve graves in the New Jerusalem.

There are twelve apostles of the Lamb in the New Testament.

Forty

Forty in Scriptures represent trials and judgment.

Jesus was tempted for forty days.

God sent rain on the earth for forty days.

God made Egypt a desolate place for forty years (Ezek. 29:11–12).

The Israelites spent forty years in the wilderness.

666

666 is the number for Satan in the Bible.

Symbology

The Bible overflows with metaphors, figurative language, symbols, and poetic language.

Symbology, the study or interpretation of symbols, therefore, is a vital part of dream interpretation. The Bible is full of symbology. We know the Holy Spirit is symbolized by a dove, by fire, by water, by rain, and by wind. Jesus is called the Lion of the Tribe of Judah, a Bridegroom, a Shepherd, the Chief Cornerstone, Bread, Light, a Vine, and the Lamb of God. Satan is symbolized by a serpent.

Here is a short list of symbols you may see in your dreams and what they mean. This list is not exhaustive, but should whet your appetite to study the Word. When you see symbols in your dreams, look for a scriptural parallel.

Bear

A bear in the Word of God is linked to deadly power (Prov. 28:15, 2 Kings 2:23–24, Dan. 7:5).

Cedars

In Scripture, cedars represent strength, pride, or cleansing.

Cedars are strong, excellent trees used to build homes and ships (2 Sam. 7:2).

Cedar wood, along with hyssop and scarlet, was used to cleanse a house (Lev. 14:49).

Dragon

Dragons represent Satan and his demons in the Bible (Isa. 27:1; 30:6, Ps. 74:13–14; Rev. 12:7–9; Ezek. 29:3; Jer. 51:34).

Milk and Honey

God spoke to the Israelites about Canaan as a land flowing with milk and honey. When the Old Testament was written, milk and honey were valuable commodities, so a land flowing with these commodities was attractive.

Beginning with Exodus 3:8, the phrase "flowing with milk and honey" appears twenty times.

When you dream of milk and honey, this can speak of provision and plenty.

Horse

In the Word of God, a horse represents strength or might in battle (Job 39:10; Ps. 147:10; Prov. 21:31).

Snakes and Serpents

Snakes and serpents are representative of Satan and his demons (Rev. 12:9; 20:2).

Stars

Stars in the Word can represent angels (Rev. 1:16; 12:4).

Thorns

Thorns can represent the cares of this world (Mark 4:18–19).

Trumpet

Trumpets in the Word are associated with sounding an alarm, offering a warning, or making an announcement (Josh. 6:4–5; Ex. 19:1–17).

Wolf

Wolves symbolize false prophets and false workers; enemies in disguise (Matt. 7:15).

Again, these are just a few of the many symbols we find in Scripture. Every symbol you find in a dream may not be so directly connected to Scripture. Remember, sometimes symbols can mean more than one thing—and sometimes they are subjective or cultural. The interpretation belongs to the Lord (Gen. 40:8). You can find 1,670 Bible symbols in the *Dictionary of Bible Themes* online, and it's free!

Dream: Walking Through the Narrow Gate

In my dream, I was at a ministry in the Midwest with which I was familiar and friendly. The church was full of millennials.

The building was remodeled with a new interior layout. To get to the sanctuary, I had to walk through a very narrow threshold. It looked like a door frame, but it was way too small to walk through comfortably.

I was thinking to myself, *I don't think I can fit through there.* I also had a slight feeling of claustrophobia, as if I might get stuck. (In reality, I'm not claustrophobic.) I pondered what to do but didn't have much time to decide. I finally made the move to go through the narrow gate because I was on assignment and had to get where I was going. However uncomfortable it was, I determined to make my way through one way or another.

I had no idea that on the other side of the narrow gate I would suddenly find myself in a huge auditorium. There was an event going on, which seemed like a major Christian concert, but it wasn't just praise and worship. There was also prayer and preaching. People were fighting and pushing to get up on the front row. I was escorted to the front.

People on the front row were sowing into the ministry randomly while the preacher was talking. The event was already under way by the time I got there, so I wasn't sure exactly what was going on. I was inquiring about what people were sowing into and how I could participate.

Suddenly, the scene shifted. Then there was a break in the event. I was with someone familiar, but I don't know who it was. We were outside. It dawned on me that I could be pregnant. I was not happy about this.

I was trying to find an easy way out of this pregnancy. I was calculating in my mind if I could take some pill and make it go away. I was looking for a way of escape. But I knew I had to birth this baby. Then I woke up.

Interpretation

This dream is a great example of how the Lord will use Bible symbols tied to Scripture but also subjective experiences to offer insight. Let's start with the millennial connection.

The Lord spoke to my heart during an extended period of worship at a house of prayer in New York City, where I was to "pour my life out as a drink offering" for the next generation. This was a verse Paul penned about his own life in relation to the body of Christ (2 Tim. 4:6; Phil. 2:17). So the fact that I was in a church that was marked by a high population of millennials was no accident. God was speaking. I believe He was saying that part of my reaching a larger segment of the body was reaching out to this underserved demographic and pouring my heart into them.

Of course, having to walk through a narrow threshold to get there immediately brought Matthew 7:13–14 to mind. I'll share this verse in the Amplified Classic translation: "Enter through the narrow gate; for wide is the gate and spacious *and* broad is the way that leads away to destruction, and many are those who are entering through it. But the gate is narrow (contracted by pressure) and the way is straitened *and* compressed that leads away to life, and few are those who find it."

Clearly, I had some concerns about going through that narrow gate, but I went anyway. The narrow way is never the easy way. It always costs you something. That I was pondering whether I could fit through the gate and dealing with fear (claustrophobia) doesn't bother me. It demonstrates a level of spiritual responsibility because the Bible tells us to count the costs (Luke 14:25–34). Fear is a normal reaction when going through transition.

If I had decided not to go through the narrow gate, then

there would have been cause for concern. But I counted the cost of answering God's call to go through this place of pressure and compression—dying to self. When I went through that passage, it seemed to shift things in the ministry. I was welcomed into places I had not been welcomed before, and I was meeting new people. It was an unfamiliar place.

In the natural, I had been praying about a sowing strategy. I believe the Lord was showing me to sow into that which is bringing me revelation in this season—to sow into ministries that are opening up the Word to me.

Now, the pregnancy dream is a theme that dates back in my life to 2004. So, there is a recurring element to this dream. I've had at least six pregnancy and baby dreams—and many others have had similar dreams about me. Being pregnant in a dream could allude to natural pregnancy but more often speaks to the birth of something new in your life, perhaps a career or a ministry—or some invention. It can speak to a promise of God that's about to manifest in your life and should bring you into a sense of expectancy. In this dream, my fleshly instinct was to look for a way out, but I knew in my heart I had to continue yielding to the Lord to birth through me what He had planted in me.

Overall, this is a good dream. The Lord is calling me to a higher level of surrender so He can use my ministry to impact more people. The grace, so to speak, is narrowed. The sowing into revelation is vital. The millennial connection is real. God used this dream to confirm many things, to provide direction into giving, to reveal yet another birthing in the ministry, and to build my faith to walk it out.

Chapter 6

CULTURAL
DREAM CODES

Traveling internationally, I've come to understand the importance of cultivating cultural awareness upon entering any
nation. When I went to Malaysia, for example, I understood ahead
of time you don't use your index finger to point because it's considered disrespectful. In America, a firm handshake is expected, but
in Asia a gentler handshake is the norm.

As you've seen by now, the dream language around the world is
not standardized, just as actual languages around the world aren't
standardized. As much as we'd like to—and as easy as it would
make it to interpret dreams—we can't fit everything we see in our
sleep into a neat little box that means the same thing to all people.

Colors, numbers, and symbols carry different connotations in different nations, ethnicities, and cultures. If you are a
Spanish speaker, for instance, God will typically not speak to you
in Chinese. If you have a dream where someone is speaking in

Chinese, it may mean something but it probably wouldn't be literal, because you have no way to even phonetically interpret the message.

Although there is an agreed upon biblical code for colors and numbers that is accurate at one level, God can go beyond these staples of dream interpretation to speak to you at a deeper level based on what colors mean to you. Like a global marketing executive, God understands what messages His people are receiving when He chooses to highlight certain colors, numbers, or symbols in dreams.

Of course, we won't go through every meaning of every color, number, and symbol in every culture here. The idea is to open your eyes to how the dream world, at least in part, can be informed by cultures. Practically speaking, God may give you a dream that includes other cultures, and one day you may need to rely on what the color means in that culture to get the fuller meaning.

Colors

Colors play a significant and sometimes unnoticed role in our lives. Colors can influence the way we think and feel. Some people in high-stress environments paint their offices blue to induce a feeling of calm. Light colors make rooms seem bigger while dark walls can make you feel like you are in a dungeon. But a color that brings you joy may trigger fear in another.

Colors carry deep meanings—but what red means in America, China, or Russia are strikingly different. Since God often chooses to speak to us through our own cultural lenses, it's helpful to understand some key distinctions, especially if you are a dream interpreter—or, again, if you are dreaming about elements in the context of different cultures. But let's look at some contrasts in various cultures to bring light to this subjectivity.

Red

In most of the Western world, red signifies love, energy, anger, or danger. In Indian cultures it can mean fear, wealth, or beauty. Yet in Asian cultures it is associated with luck.

Blue

In North American culture, blue can indicate sadness or depression, or trust and peace. In Eastern Europe it connotes healing. And among the Indian culture, it speaks of immorality.

Green

In the West, green can suggest jealousy (on the negative side) or prosperity (on the positive side). It can also point to environmental issues.

Middle Eastern cultures use green as a symbol of their prophet Muhammad.

But in Asia it can mean anything from eternity and fertility to infidelity and vitality.

Yellow

In Europe, yellow stands for weakness, betrayal, or jealousy. In North American culture, though, yellow can translate to cowardice, but it also speaks of joy and hope.

In Greece, yellow means sadness and, similarly, in Burma it is the color associated with mourning.

Pink

Eastern nations use pink to suggest femininity, but in Belgium pink is traditionally associated with baby boys.

In Thailand pink is associated with Tuesday, and in Korea pink speaks of trust.

In most of the world, though, pink is a fairly standard color to represent love, romance, and femininity.

Orange

We see a wide range of cultural nuances with the color orange. For example, in the Netherlands orange is the color of the Royal Dutch family.

In Ireland it's a religious color for Protestants, while in Thailand it's the color associated with Thursday.

In the West, orange speaks of Halloween or safety in hunting and construction zones. Yet in many Eastern countries it takes on spiritual meanings or stands for joy.

Purple

Purple stands for royalty, high ranks, and military honors (think Purple Heart) in the Western world.

Purple has a similar connotation in the East, where it is associated with wealth.

But in India, it is indicative of sorrow. In Brazil, death or mourning.

Brown

In China, brown is the color of the earth, but in India it is associated with mourning.

In the West, brown symbolizes stability, dependability, and being down-to-earth.

Specifically in Nicaragua, brown stands for disapproval.

White

In the West, white speaks of purity, peace, weddings, and the like.

That's a stark contrast to the Eastern cultures, where white marks death, funerals, mourning, and sadness.

In China, it can mean all these things and more, including misfortune, age, and humility.

White also has negative connotations in India and Japan.

Black

Meanwhile, black is a power color in the West, while it also stands for funerals, mourning, and death.

In the Eastern world, black stands for health, wealth, and prosperity, but in India it means anger, evil, darkness, and other measures of negativity.

You can see from this exercise in comparison and contrast how the interpretation of a dream could be vastly different from one culture to the next based on a single color. Although the interpretation belongs to God, He often speaks to people through the lens of their culture, and colors play a significant role.

Numbers

Thirteen

Numbers carry good, bad, and ugly meanings in various cultures around the world. If you live in the West, for example, you know thirteen is considered an "unlucky" number. We don't build thirteenth floors in buildings, and we don't like Friday the thirteenth. Even horror movies have been named after that infamous day.

How powerful is this number in the minds of some? The term *friggatriskaidekaphobia* was created to describe it—it is defined as fear of Friday the thirteenth. According to the Stress Management Center and Phobia Institute, fear of Friday the thirteenth affects around 17 million Americans. Nobody even really knows why so many dread this day. But in Italy the number thirteen is lucky.

It's interesting to make the point about numbers in culture by exploring bad luck numbers in various nations or regions of the world. While I personally don't believe in bad luck, that doesn't bear on how God may speak subjectively to people—even you—through numbers.

Four

Let's start with China. Four in Chinese sounds almost like the word "death." Like the thirteenth floor is left off the elevator schemata in America, Chinese buildings often ignore the fourth floor. But in Germany the number is lucky. In the Western world, a four-leaf clover is a symbol of good luck, with the four leaves representing hope, faith, love, and luck.

Nine, Thirty-nine

In Japan, the number nine carries a negative connotation. That may be simply because the number nine in Japanese sounds a lot like the word "torture." In fact, some hospitals and airlines in Japan refuse to use the number nine because of the impression it leaves on the minds of people they serve. If a Japanese dreamer has the number nine show up in their dream life, it may speak to them of a tormenting situation. But nine is considered a lucky number in China and Norway. Head over to Afghanistan and people are averse to the number 39 because the word for this number sounds like *morda-gow*, which means dead cow.

Seventeen

In Italy, the number seventeen carries a negative connotation that dates all the way back to Roman numeral inceptions. Seventeen in Roman numerals is XVII. That's an anagram—a word that becomes another word when you mix up the letters, like the word dormitory rearranged to read dirty room—of VIXI. VIXI means "I lived" in Latin and is often found on tombstones like Rest in Peace (or RIP) in the United States. So, if a Roman dreams of the number seventeen, they may associate that with death.

191, 26

Speaking of the United States, 191 has now taken on a strong undertone of doom. In the United States aviation world, 191 is an unlucky number because five individual flights numbered 191 crashed. So if an aviator dreamed of the number 191, that would mean something much different to him than it might mean to someone else. Travel over to India and you find a different number associated with tragic events—26. As culturists tell it, India has seen natural disasters—including earthquakes and tsunamis—as well as terrorist attacks on the twenty-sixth day of various months over the past fifteen years. So, if someone in India dreams of the number 26, it could send a chill down their spine.

Eight

Bulgaria has its own issue with numbers—and a strange one. The phone number 0888888888 speaks of a jinx or a curse because people in their society who had that number all died an untimely death. Apparently, this notion started when a Bulgarian mobile phone company owner with this string of eights in his identifier died of cancer. Another person with that number was apparently shot and another assassinated. That phone number was taken off the market in Bulgaria, but someone who dreams of a string of eights could get scared to death about what might happen next. In India, eight is also an unwelcome sight because it stands for broken peace or relationships.

Strings of Eights, Threes, Sixes

In both Japan and China, a string of eights is a good sign. It's a lucky number because when you say it aloud it sounds like prosperity or wealth. Three threes are a strategic number set for Swedes. In Sweden, they have a saying, "all good things come in groups of three." This is in contrast to the belief in America that "bad things happen in threes." A lucky number in China is 666, which tends to mean "everything goes smoothly." However, in Christian cultures 666 is a demonic number associated with the Antichrist.

Seven, Three, Fifteen, Odd and Even Numbers

The number seven is known as a lucky number in cultures around the world—typically in the West. In the United Kingdom, Netherlands, France, and America, seven is celebrated, whereas in many Asian nations it's an unwelcome sight. Three is also a lucky number in Italy and China. The number fifteen is often celebrated in Spanish speaking countries. Even numbers are avoided in Russia while odd numbers speak of good things.

Animals

Whether or not you are an animal lover, you've surely recognized some animals are celebrated and others are shunned in various cultures of the world.

Dogs

In America, we like to say dogs are man's best friend. But in countries like China, Korea, and Vietnam, they eat dog meat for dinner. It's worthwhile to explore the cultural meanings of various animals in the context of dream interpretation.

Bats and Bears

Although Batman is a popular superhero in the United States, the bat symbolizes death and witchcraft in many cultures. Movies like Dracula have informed American views of bats, but in China bats are a symbol of joy and luck. In American culture, bears have symbolized friendly companions—Smokey the Bear, teddy bears, Winnie the Pooh, and so on. Although bears can be fierce and scary, most cultures around the world have a positive view of bears.

Monkeys

Monkeys are often associated with curiosity (remember Curious George?), playfulness, and intelligence in the West. In China, monkeys symbolize friendship. In Buddhist teachings, monkeys symbolize courage. In Mexico, monkeys are associated with the arts. Can you see how vastly different the meaning of a monkey could be in the dreams of people with different cultural backgrounds? Although it's all positive, the interpretations from dreamers in these various cultures could be much different.

Birds and Butterflies

Just as many types of birds appear in dreams—from parrots to roosters to eagles and beyond—there are many different views of birds in cultures around the world. Butterflies can mean many things to many people. In China and Greece, for example, butterflies speak of eternal life. But in Japan butterflies can represent the soul of someone who has died. In Celtic religions butterflies symbolize joy, honor, and prosperity, while in Christianity they speak of resurrection and transformation.

Likewise, in some cultures a dove represents the soul of man, but in Christianity the dove is a symbol of the Holy Spirit. Continuing the bird theme, eagles in Christianity represent prophetic ministry. In many cultures, an owl is a symbol of wisdom, but owls can also be associated with the occult and witchcraft.

Bulls, Cats, and Tigers

Bulls can speak of stubbornness in American culture or male virility in Asian cultures. Royalty marks the bull in Egypt, while the bull speaks of energy in India. Cats represent bad luck in many cultures—specifically black cats. Cats are considered symbols of evil in Egypt, a symbol of disease in Europe, and a sacred animal in Thailand. Tigers speak of power and passion in Asian cultures.

Snakes and Spiders

Cleary, snakes represent evil as far back as the book of Genesis when the snake tempted Eve in the garden of Eden and opened the door for the fall of man (Gen. 3). Snakes can also represent seduction, lies, and poison. But in India some snakes—like the cobra—are revered. So, if an American dreams of a cobra it would represent some manner of evil, whereas an Indian would take away a much different meaning. Spiders can also be associated with witchcraft, but some cultures see them as representative of creativity or even good luck.

Horses, Foxes, and Lions

Horses can represent anything from strength to stamina to friendship in various cultures of the world. Christians see foxes as something that "spoils the vine" (Song 2:15), but the Japanese connect foxes with wealth. By contrast, Chinese see the devil in a fox. Christians see lions as either symbolic of the Lord or the enemy, depending on the context. Either way, lions are still associated with courage, strength, and royalty. Lions are widely known across cultures as "the king of the jungle."

This is not meant to be an exhaustive study but the point is that what an animal means to you may be different to someone in another culture. If you are diving into dream interpretation, cultural nuances are something to strongly consider. Just as you would not travel to a nation without understanding the customs, you shouldn't interpret a dream without understanding the varied symbols.

Serious and Silly Superstitions

Interpreting dreams in a cultural context also means understanding superstitions. You've probably heard things like "step on a crack, and you'll break your mother's back." If you have a dream where you are stomping on cracks while you are feeling upset with your mother, is God trying to tell you something or is that your soul? As you can see, there are many layers to dream interpretation. But in any context, the superstitions we've been taught or exposed to—whether we believe them or not—can inform our dreams.

Knock on Wood

In the world of superstition, knocking on wood is a way to prevent a jinx or curse. If you are knocking on wood in a dream, a superstition that dates back to medieval times, it could mean you are looking for divine guidance, or it could mean you are depending on something else other than God to guide you. This is where, again, you have to explore the entire context of the dream, the players, your emotions, and other elements. The origin of knocking on wood actually comes from the church world. European believers supposedly touched the wood from Christ's cross to feel a connection to God.

Black Cats

We know cats are associated with evil and witchcraft in most cultures, so it's no wonder a superstition formed about bad luck occurring if a black cat crosses your path.

Birds

When crows show up on the scene, South Koreans see it as bad luck—even a sign that death is in the air. In Europe ravens are considered bad luck. Birds also represent death in some cultures when they fly into your house and land on a chair, then fly away.

Mirrors

When your mirror cracks it means seven years of bad luck in the world of bad omens. If you have a dream where there is a cracked mirror, though, it doesn't mean God is saying bad luck is your portion. It could have to do with a crack in the foundation of your identity, or a fracture in your understanding of who you are in Christ. Don't let superstition interpret your dreams apart from the Spirit of God, but understand that God could use a deeply ingrained cultural superstition to communicate something to you.

Trimming Your Nails at Night

This may seem ridiculous to you, but trimming your fingernails or toenails after dark is considered bad luck in South Korea, India, Turkey, and Japan. It speaks to danger or even death.

Chewing Gum at Night

Chewing gum at night is morbid in Turkey. Superstition has it that the gum turns into the flesh of dead people. Clearly, a dream of chewing gum at night would mean something much different to a Turkish person than an Australian.

Leaving Things on the Ground

In Russia, leaving bottles on the ground represents good luck whereas in Brazil if you leave your wallet or purse on the ground it's a bad financial omen.

Water

In Serbia, spilling water behind someone is a blessing, but in Germany toasting with water is associated with death.

Whistling

The *Snow White and the Seven Dwarfs* song "Whistle While You Work" would not sit well in Russia or Norway. That's because whistling, especially whistling indoors, opens the door to financial hardship in Russia and brings unwanted rain in Norway.

Superstitions abound, and space does not permit us to explore them all. A few worth noting, in case they should appear in your dreams or the dreams of those you're helping to offer understanding, include: sitting at the corner of a table; the evil eye; Tuesday the thirteenth, Argentinian werewolves; saying the word "rabbit" on the first day of the month; pennies; walking backwards; opening scissors without cutting anything; tucking in your thumbs at a cemetery; yellow flowers; white ribbons; manhole covers inscribed with the letters A or K; women eating goat meat; sleeping with a fan on; and eating grapes on New Year's Eve.

Symbols

When I travel around the world, I see symbols—from traffic signs to religious marks and beyond. By definition, a symbol is something that stands for or suggests something else by reason of relationship, association, convention, or accidental resemblance, according to *Merriam-Webster*'s dictionary. A symbol communicates what words express.

Language itself is marked by symbols, which we call letters but nonverbal symbols, such as hand gestures and facial expressions, can also speak loudly. Graphic symbols like the swastika or an upside-down cross can engender strong emotions. While some symbols are unique to specific cultures, which we'll explore in short in the paragraphs ahead, some symbols mean one thing in the West and something entirely different in the East. The hexagram is a prime example. In the West, we see this as the Star of David. In the East, Hindus use the hexagram symbol to represent unity between God and man or between man and woman.

The "Hook 'Em Horns"—a hand gesture by which you hold up your pinky and forefinger while the other digits of your hands are pointed down—stands for the University of Texas mascot. It's supposed to symbolize the head and horns of cattle. But in Europe it represents satanism. That's an incredibly vast swing in symbology. This hand gesture in a dream, then, would mean something far more sinister to a Londoner than a Texan. The infinity symbol, which looks like an eight laid on its side, is a mathematical representation of a numerical unit that has no end. But in certain religions, like Hinduism and Buddhism, it represents reincarnation.

The Bible is full of symbology. Since symbology is distinct in various cultures around the world, it's vital to understand how these ethnic and national symbols translate to the dream world. Let's look at some interesting symbols from around the world and how they might inform your dream life—or a dream you are working with the Spirit of God to interpret for someone else.

Hand Gestures

We've already discussed horn fingers. Beyond the University of Texas, music enthusiasts in the United States use it to mean "rock on." And beyond a sign for satanism, in some parts of the world—typically Latin American countries—this is a sign to tell a man his wife is cheating on him. The "okay" sign indicates agreement in the United States, United Kingdom, Canada, and Australia. But that hand sign turned upside down means something vulgar in Brazil.

Giving a "thumbs up" is a sign of approval in Russia, Canada, the United States, the United Kingdom, and Australia. But it means something vulgar in Switzerland and France. Crossed fingers represent a hope for good luck in Australia, the United States, the United Kingdom, and Canada but represents something lewd in Vietnam. The "V" sign means peace in the United States but represents defiance in the United Kingdom, Ireland, New Zealand, and Australia. The list of hand symbols goes on and on. As you can see, the meanings vary widely.

Facial Expressions

Some facial expressions are the same across cultures. You can see joy or anger on someone's face, for example. But winking means different things in different cultures. In Latin America, for example, it's considered flirting. In the United States it can mean you are joking, while in West Africa when an adult winks at a child, it signals they are to leave the room.

Body Language

Beyond facial expressions and hand gestures is broader body language. Remember, everything means something in a dream. Your posture or someone else's posture can herald truth you may not discern in your waking hours. Crossing your arms over your chest, for example, suggests being closed off from others. Closed postures—postures in which people are covering parts of their body—can indicate one who feels guarded or even hostile. More open postures, by contrast, communicate a welcoming, friendly, inviting tone. Slouching can represent laziness or disrespect. Leaning forward communicates interest and attentiveness. Just as postures communicate something in real life, body language also communicates in dreams.

Good Luck Symbols

Good luck symbols vary around the world. In the United States, lady bugs are considered signs of good luck and prosperity, while in China that role belongs to the cricket. Dream catchers represent good luck in Native American culture, but in the Christian world they speak of the occult. In Chinese culture a red lantern symbolizes good luck, but in the West a horseshoe does. Ladders, keys, horns, triangles, wheels, and many other objects speak to "luck" in various cultures. The context of your dream matters. If you find yourself in another country in your dream—like Japan— the symbols you see may mean something different than what you normally would think. Explore this with the Holy Spirit.

Status Symbols

In America, luxury homes, cars, yachts, jewelry, and fine clothing are considered status symbols. Not so in other countries. In some Asian nations, like Malaysia, Thailand, and Indonesia, teenagers wear fake braces on their teeth as a status symbol. Drinking Starbucks coffee, which comes at a premium cost there, is somewhat of a status symbol. In Africa, high body mass and smartphones are considered status symbols. In the context of a dream, if you are in China drinking Starbucks, that could mean the Lord is speaking to you about provision for a project or ministry there. If you are interpreting a dream for someone with an African cultural background, a smartphone could be a symbol of coming provision.

As you can see, symbols have deeply ingrained—and sometimes opposite—meanings in the cultures and people groups of the world. They can also have contrasting meanings in your dream life and the dream lives of those sharing their nighttime revelations with you. Our role in responsibly interpreting dreams is to take the time to research symbols in context and, as I have said over and again in this book, to understand that the interpretation belongs to the Lord (Gen. 40:8).

Chapter 7

SUBJECTIVE
DREAM CODES

G od speaks to us in ways that are personal. Any two given
people in the world—or even in a household—could have
very similar dreams and accurately draw two entirely different
meanings based on a variety of personal factors.

Here's a great example: If you are a dog lover, God may use a
dog in your dream to symbolize loyalty. But if you were attacked
by dogs as a youth, a dog will mean something much different to
you—old Fido would not be a welcomed sight. In other words,
dream codes are subjective. Here's another example: If you have
been through a painful divorce, a dream in which you are getting married may mean something totally different to you than to
someone who is longing for a mate. And marriage doesn't always
mean actual marriage. It could mean a covenant or partnership.
Again, it's subjective.

By subjective, I mean particular to your worldview. We all have
personal preferences—even biases. We have unique background

and life experiences. Even within the same family, parents relate to individual children in subjective ways. A dad may relate differently to his son than his daughter; differently to his firstborn than his last born based on their personalities or what he has learned over the years.

God knows our emotional makeup better than we do. God knows our knowledge base. God knows our personal experiences. And He knows we're going to filter any and all communications through a uniquely-colored lens. While we must always turn to the Bible for interpretation, sometimes the interpretation is more subjective than biblical—but will never violate Scripture.

Dreams, then, are not only symbolic and parabolic, at times they are subjective. When you are interpreting dreams other people have—whether it's about you or about something related to your own life—you can't filter it through your own dream code. Our heavenly Father speaks to us in a way that is intimate; therefore each person has a unique one-on-one with God.

The Butler and the Baker

In Genesis 40, we find ourselves in a prison scene. Joseph was already sentenced to jail after a false accusation came against him in Potiphar's house. He was there when Pharaoh got angry with two of his attendants—the chief butler and the chief baker—and tossed them into the prison with Joseph. Consider this passage, starting with Genesis 40:5–13 NKJV:

> Then the butler and the baker of the king of Egypt, who were confined in the prison, had a dream, both of them, each man's

dream in one night and each man's dream with its own interpretation. And Joseph came in to them in the morning and looked at them, and saw that they were sad. So he asked Pharaoh's officers who were with him in the custody of his lord's house, saying, "Why do you look so sad today?"

And they said to him, "We each have had a dream, and there is no interpreter of it."

So Joseph said to them, "Do not interpretations belong to God? Tell them to me, please."

Then the chief butler told his dream to Joseph, and said to him, "Behold, in my dream a vine was before me, and in the vine were three branches; it was as though it budded, its blossoms shot forth, and its clusters brought forth ripe grapes. Then Pharaoh's cup was in my hand; and I took the grapes and pressed them into Pharaoh's cup, and placed the cup in Pharaoh's hand."

And Joseph said to him, "This is the interpretation of it: The three branches are three days. Now within three days Pharaoh will lift up your head and restore you to your place, and you will put Pharaoh's cup in his hand according to the former manner, when you were his butler."

Let's pause here. Notice the numerology in this passage. The number three is significant. In this case, three wasn't merely some Bible correlation; there was a literal interpretation. We'll study more about numbers in a later chapter. Bible numerology is a complex symbolic language, but sometimes numbers have a quite literal meaning.

There was also symbology in the above passage, but it was subjective to the chief butler's profession. Some Bible translations call him the cupbearer. This man tasted the king's food and wine before serving it to him to make sure it was acceptable and not poisoned. So the branches, blossoms, and grapes also carried a highly important message. Beyond the numbers, there's also the literal interpretation of the cupbearer serving the king in the dream. All of this pointed to his restoration.

Now let's look at the chief baker's dream and interpretation, which we find in Genesis 40:16–19 NKJV:

> When the chief baker saw that the interpretation was good, he said to Joseph, "I also was in my dream, and there were three white baskets on my head. In the uppermost basket were all kinds of baked goods for Pharaoh, and the birds ate them out of the basket on my head." So Joseph answered and said, "This is the interpretation of it: The three baskets are three days. Within three days Pharaoh will lift off your head from you and hang you on a tree; and the birds will eat your flesh from you."

Peter's Vision of the Sheets

In Acts 10:9–16 NKJV, we see the concept of subjectivity in visions, but this can just as well apply to the dream world. Read carefully how Peter's bias is revealed and challenged in this passage:

> The next day, as they went on their journey and drew near the city, Peter went up on the housetop to pray, about the sixth hour. Then he became very hungry and wanted to eat; but while they made ready, he fell into a trance and saw heaven opened and an object like a great sheet bound at the four corners, descending

to him and let down to the earth. In it were all kinds of four-footed animals of the earth, wild beasts, creeping things, and birds of the air. And a voice came to him, "Rise, Peter; kill and eat." But Peter said, "Not so, Lord! For I have never eaten anything common or unclean." And a voice spoke to him again the second time, "What God has cleansed you must not call common." This was done three times. And the object was taken up into heaven again.

Just after this, men came from the house of Cornelius, a Gentile. They beckoned Peter to come to Cornelius. Peter agreed, due to the vision, and Cornelius's household was saved and baptized in the Holy Spirit. God ultimately used this vision to challenge and overcome Peter's biases, but also the biases of the early Jewish believers who at that time thought salvation was only for the Jews.

Matthew Henry's Commentary explains:

The prejudices of Peter against the Gentiles, would have prevented his going to Cornelius, unless the Lord had prepared him for this service. To tell a Jew that God had directed those animals to be reckoned clean which were hitherto deemed unclean, was in effect saying, that the law of Moses was done away. Peter was soon made to know the meaning of it. God knows what services are before us, and how to prepare us; and we know the meaning of what he has taught us, when we find what occasion we have to make use of it.

In this passage and commentary, we clearly see how our personal biases can impact how we receive or reject dreams or visions that are distinctly from God. At first, Peter actually resisted the

Lord in this vision. How many of us have tossed out true dreams from the Lord due to our own personal biases? This passage makes me wonder.

From this passage we also learn that God can use dreams and visions, as He did with Peter, to correct our biases. Bias means, "an inclination of temperament or outlook; especially: a personal and sometimes unreasoned judgment," according to *Merriam-Webster*'s dictionary. It also means a bent or tendency.

Our biases affect how we perceive information. God knows this, so He will, at times, speak to us with our biases in mind. If you are a sports lover, God may use sports metaphors in your dreams that would mean nothing to someone else. If you have an affinity or bias toward a certain people group—whether by culture, race, age, religion, whatever—the symbols or storylines in your dream will mean something different to you than someone else.

Do you know what your biases are? Now is a good time to ask the Lord. Everyone has biases, most of them are subconscious. They were learned or shaped by life experience. It's not necessarily always a negative thing. When you bias the Word of God in a dark culture, it's a good thing. Likewise, when your bias is toward loyalty and integrity, these are strong values.

You may never fully know all of your biases, and you certainly don't know all of another's biases. Therefore, we must conclude that dream interpretation has subjective elements and that the interpretation still belongs to God (Gen. 40:8). Take a lesson from Peter's vision. If something strikes you hard as ungodly or wrong in a dream, ask the Lord if He's trying to tear down some of your biases.

Paul's Night Vision About the Macedonian

Paul's vision during the night about the man in Macedonia is telling. Notice how the Holy Spirit forbid them twice from entering certain regions before the Macedonian call:

> Now when they had gone through Phrygia and the region of Galatia, they were forbidden by the Holy Spirit to preach the word in Asia. After they had come to Mysia, they tried to go into Bithynia, but the Spirit did not permit them. So passing by Mysia, they came down to Troas. And a vision appeared to Paul in the night. A man of Macedonia stood and pleaded with him, saying, "Come over to Macedonia and help us." Now after he had seen the vision, immediately we sought to go to Macedonia, concluding that the Lord had called us to preach the gospel to them. (Acts 16:6–10 NKJV)

Paul, who was intimate with the Holy Spirit and heard clearly from the Lord, must have felt he was supposed to go to Asia and Bithynia—but the Holy Spirit had other plans. The Macedonian call answered what questions he surely had about the redirections. Up until this point, Paul's missionary journeys had focused on the East. Now, God was calling him into the West. The Holy Spirit was commissioning Paul to take the gospel to new nations. Like Peter with the mind-set of taking the gospel to the Jews only, Paul had a mind to stay in the East until the Holy Spirit opened his eyes. The Macedonian call changed Paul's ministry, making it truly global.

How Emotions Can Impact Our Dreams

When it comes to discussion of subjectivity in dreams, it's worth looking at the world of emotions. Your emotions are subjective to you. No one but God truly understands how you feel about various situations—for good or bad—in your dreams.

Our soul contains our mind, will, and emotions. Emotions can fluctuate in any given season and even on any given day. We are capable of being very angry one day, then letting it go the next day—or even angry in one moment and peaceful in the next. We can be thrilled with good news, but the ecstatic feelings of happiness don't remain long-term. They may give way to some other circumstantial emotion. You may experience a season of grief after a major loss, but those feelings will eventually pass.

Emotions come and go, and the dreams we receive during different emotional states add a layer of subjectivity to your dreams. God understands our emotional state. Through your dreams, God can reveal to you emotions that you've stuffed down into the recesses of your soul. He can show you hidden fears in your dreams. He can reveal sinful attitudes in dreams. By the same token, your daytime fears can impact your nightly dreams. Your daytime anger can drive dreams with frustrating circumstances. These dreams are soulish dreams where you are processing your feelings through your subconscious.

You can also feel emotions in dreams in response to what you are seeing or hearing in that dream state. These emotions may not reside in your soul but be contained in the dream itself. For example, you find yourself in a dream meeting the man or woman you are going to marry and feeling love, peace, and joy. Or you may find yourself in a dream seeing someone die and feel grief.

When you wake up, you may not feel those same emotions because you realize the dream is not real. But the emotions were real in the dream—and they mean something.

Science confirms emotions impact how we communicate and, more importantly in this context, how we receive communications. If you are angry and upset, you don't want to hear more bad news. If you are on an emotional high, you don't want to hear bad news either, but how you filter that bad news in these two emotional states differs. The angry person who receives bad news may fly into a rage. The emotionally elated person who receives bad news may see it as a temporary situation and more readily find a solution.

God understands how our emotional state filters communication and is able to speak to us clearly despite the filters. Interpreting what He is saying, though, is a different story. When we're in various emotional states, we can easily misinterpret what God is saying to us. This is when we need to subject our dreams to others who are wise in the Lord or who have the gift of dream interpretation for help. This is also why it's important to write down every detail of the dream to review later. You may interpret it one way now, but when your emotions settle you may see what God is really trying to say.

God can also settle our emotions in a dream. If we're walking through a season of loneliness or grief, He can comfort us in a dream and soothe those feelings. If we are walking through a season of frustration, He can show us positive outcomes according to His will to stir our faith. If we are walking through a season of denial, He can show us what we need to see so that we can face it, accept it, and move on.

Understanding the concept of emotional intelligence is helpful in the realm of understanding subjective dream codes. According to the Institute for Health and Human Potential, "Emotional Intelligence (EQ or EI) is a term created by two researchers—Peter Salavoy and John Mayer—and popularized by Dan Goleman in his 1996 book of the same name. We define EI as the ability to: recognize, understand and manage our own emotions; recognize, understand and influence the emotions of others. In practical terms, this means being aware that emotions can drive our behavior and impact people (positively and negatively), and learning how to manage those emotions—both our own and others—especially when we are under pressure."[15]

As Christians, we should never let our emotions lead us. Romans 8:14 NKJV tells us, "For as many as are led by the Spirit of God, these are sons of God." Emotions do have a bearing in the world of subjective dream interpretation, and we should be aware of our emotional state, but the interpretation still belongs to the Lord (Gen. 40:8). Whatever emotions surface in or after a dream—or whatever the Lord shows you about your emotions in a dream—submit it to the Lord. Inquire of the Lord as to what He is showing you.

Dream: Traveling to the Florida Keys

Some dreams are long and complex, but easy to interpret. Other dreams are short and more difficult to interpret. I had a short dream that was full of meaning many might miss on the surface.

In the dream, I was trying to get down to the Florida Keys. My mother and father were with me. Confusion and urgency were the main feelings I had throughout the dream. I was running late. I was driving in a Triumph Spitfire. I had to cross the salt water in the car. I wasn't sure why we couldn't use the bridge that takes you from South Miami through the Florida Keys all the way down to Key West. I just know we had to scramble to find an alternate route. My father gave us the strategy to drive the car through the water. My mother rode with me in the car.

In the dream, I was concerned about the car engine getting flooded and was driving fast, hoping to make it through before the car engine quit.

There are many subjective elements in this dream worth noting, but there are also heart issues revealed, assignments unlocked, and opposition outlined. Indeed, this dream is thick with layers of revelation.

Let's start with the nature of the journey. I was trying to get down to the Florida Keys. I am a native Floridian and have been down to the Keys many times. I know the journey. It's actually a very short distance from where I live—less than 200 miles—but it can take four or five hours to drive to the bottom of the Keys, depending on the traffic, because of the very narrow road and low speed limit. It's a time investment to get to Key West.

Keys in this context seem to represent opportunity; God's will. There was a lot of confusion. We know God is not the author of confusion (1 Cor. 14:33), so this confusion was clearly not from God. There was also urgency, which was likely from the Lord. It's been said the Lord is never in a hurry, but I believe when He has a task or assignment for us to perform, He's not in the habit of sitting still. Urgency is not a bad thing—it speaks to a call for immediate attention. There is a kairos time—a God-ordained time—for some assignments. The enemy was bringing confusion in the midst of urgency, which caused me to run late.

In this dream, I was in a hurry. Your emotions or state of

mind in a dream are telling. I felt this urgency, this need to hurry, which could signify a strong feeling to get prepared for the journey ahead. It could also signal the impending birth of a ministry. When a pregnant woman's water breaks, there is an urgency to get to the hospital because the clock has started ticking. Birth is inevitable at that point. The woman must do the final preparations to bring new life into the world. My hurried state in the dream could also mean I needed to make a decision quickly. I seem to have already decided to go after the keys, but I was running late.

In the dream, I felt like I was going to miss out if I did not hurry. Naturally speaking, this shows that I felt I would miss a God opportunity if I did not act swiftly to move forward. Running in this context speaks of my eagerness and commitment to the plan. So, we can discern I was eager and committed to getting into God's will, but there was confusion and resistance; therefore I needed to take an alternate route.

Next, I was driving a Triumph Spitfire, a small British sports car. This is subjective to me as this is the type of car I drove when I was in high school. Cars have to do with ministry or career. The Triumph is also a foreign car, indicating I was not familiar with the situation in which I found myself.

I did some research to gain insight into the dream. The definition of triumph, according to *Merriam-Webster's* dictionary, is "to gain a victory; be victorious; win; to gain mastery; prevail; to triumph over fear; to be successful; achieve success; to exult over victory; rejoice over success; to be elated or glad; rejoice proudly; glory." With this definition, I looked up Scriptures dealing with triumph and found the following:

Psalm 25:2: "O my God, I trust in You; may I not be
ashamed; may my enemies not triumph over me."

Psalm 59:10: "The God of lovingkindness will go before me;
God will cause me to look in triumph on my enemies."

Psalm 118:7: "The Lord is on my side to help me; I shall look
in triumph upon those who hate me."

2 Corinthians 2:14: "Now thanks be to God who always
causes us to triumph in Christ and through us reveals
the fragrance of His knowledge in every place."

Colossians 2:15–16: "And having disarmed authorities
and powers, He (Jesus) made a show of them openly,
triumphing over them by the cross."

Every one of those Scriptures is in the context of enemy opposition, which is telling. God was showing me He was going to give me triumph over the enemies that were working to prevent me from getting the keys.

Also, through natural study I discovered the Spitfire is a British fighter plane with a single in-line engine used by the R.A.F. throughout World War II. This is significant because it is good for warfare—in my case, spiritual warfare! Spit can represent the anointing, as when Jesus spit and made mud to put on the blind man's eyes to heal him. And fire is a symbol of the presence of God or the glory of God. I was driving an anointed, glorious, and fire warfare car to victory! Hallelujah!

Digging deeper, my father in this dream represented my heavenly Father. My mother in this dream represented the Holy Spirit. The Father was directing me with a strategy. The Holy Spirit was accompanying me in the car. The divine strategy to skirt the enemy was to drive through the water as an alternate route. It was a change in the traditional path one would take. It could signify moving to the next level of glory on a path less traveled due to resistance. I was on an alternate path; I was taking an unusual way. Water is a symbol of the Holy Spirit, and we were in salt water, which speaks of preservation.

In the dream, I was concerned about the engine flooding. An engine is what drives forward-moving motion. I was concerned the enemy's flood would stall the engine. Floods can be symbols of verbal assaults from the enemy. So there was some fear to overcome in this battle for the new opportunity. But while processing this dream, the Lord brought this Scripture to mind: "When you pass through the waters, I will be with you; and through the rivers, they will not overflow you. When you walk through the fire, you will not be scorched, nor will the flame burn you" (Isa. 43:2 NASB).

God assured me the victory in this dream, and that is what I held on to when the spiritual battle ensued over the keys He was trying to put into my hands.

Chapter 8

INTERPRETING DREAMS WITH GOD'S WISDOM

I n one of the most disturbing dreams I have had, I walked into the prayer room at my ministry and it was dark. That wasn't altogether unusual because during the worship time on Friday night corporate prayer the lights are often dimmed. In the dream, I saw two men on the platform I did not recognize. They were dressed in black.

When I scanned the prayer room I saw someone had a pillow and was sleeping at the altar. I wasn't sure exactly what was going on. *Is this a prayer lock-in?* I wondered. Suddenly I received the bad news that someone had died. In the dream, I did not know who it was. I was so shaken that two people had to help me leave the prayer room and exit the building. Then I woke up.

We need to decipher every dream with God's wisdom, but an especially disturbing dream or a directional dream demands extra caution. When your emotions are very stirred in a dream—so stirred that you wake up disturbed and have a hard time shaking the feeling—you need to pay extra attention to what the Lord is trying to show you. At the same time, emotions can get in the way of discernment.

Immediately, as I began to interpret this dream, I wondered if someone in the ministry was going to die. I was so shaken up by the dream that my mind immediately thought of physical death. Before the end of the day, I received a call from someone pivotal in my ministry with bad news: his young son had been diagnosed with cancer.

I wondered if the dream was about the boy. Was the Lord showing me there was a death assignment against the boy? I prayed but did not bear witness to this interpretation.

So I continued to pray. I wondered if the dream was about the boy's father, the department leader. Would he leave the ministry to care for his son? Are we losing this leader? Was it about a relational death rather than a physical death? I understood that death in a dream doesn't always mean physical death. It can also mean spiritual death, dying to self, the death of a career, relationship, ministry, or even some sort of judgment or separation.

God's wisdom always keeps the context in mind. The context of this dream was not personal—it was ministry. As I prayed and began to unravel the dream, it became clear this was not about a physical death or the death of the ministry but about the death of a ministry relationship. Although the leader whose son was battling cancer did slowly move away from the ministry, there was not a death in this relationship. Yet I was convinced the death of a relationship was coming. I just had no idea how soon.

I knew I had to pray because I was so visibly shaken in the dream. The Lord used that dream to prepare me for what was coming—to pray to guard my heart. The pillow in the dream represented resting in faith and in the context of the prayer room it translated to me as resting in faith through prayer. So I prayed for God to help me brace myself for what was about to happen. I refused to become fearful about it. I refused to dread what was coming. I kept the matter in my heart and considered it from time to time, but I did not let it consume me.

It was less than two months before this dream came to pass. While I was putting the ministry in order, I moved some people to different positions and asked others to take a break for a season while we reorganized. One woman was offended and hurt by the reorganization and not only left the ministry but also severed a friendship that was nearly two decades old. This could have been devastating for me on a personal level, but it wasn't—because God had prepared me through my dream.

What would normally have been a very emotional separation—an overwhelming emotional shock—surprised me but did not stir me at all. God warned me ahead of time and my response was to pray. If I had ignored or misinterpreted the dream, the personal outcome would have been different. I would have been shocked and emotionally wounded. But I responded correctly to the dream, and God protected me.

There was another aspect to this dream that I could not grasp until after the dream was fulfilled: the two strangers in black. I believed from the beginning these were evil spirits. I pondered, studied, and prayed about these two men in black for weeks and could not get any clear understanding of what spirits these signified. During the transition, two people were offended and left the ministry. A spirit of offense was talking to these people and tempted them to leave when their positions shifted.

I moved through the interpretation of that dream with the Spirit of God, navigating it bit by bit. I tackled each layer, exploring things in prayer. Read the dream and the interpretation again and notice how some of the interpretation process was trial and error.

Finally, parts of the dream were not clear until after the dream manifested. The Lord showed me after the fact what spirits were involved. Was He trying to warn me about the spirit of offense beforehand so I could pray against it? Perhaps. Maybe I missed that part. I still don't know. But I do know that after the people left the ministry—after this pruning—there was great growth. What the enemy meant for harm, God used for good (Gen. 50:20).

Steps to Interpreting Dreams with God

Let's explore steps to interpreting dreams with God's wisdom. If you'll use these steps as a guideline—and stay prayerful—you will be well on your way to decoding your dreams.

Write Down the Dream

I can't stress this enough—write down your dreams. Write them down and judge them later. In chapter 11, we'll explore extensive reasons for and benefits of writing down your dreams. Even if a dream is from your soul or from the enemy, it can be useful. Dreams reveal things about ourselves or about the enemy's plans for our lives that we might otherwise not see or understand.

Judge the Dream

We've already discussed at length the sources of dreams. Dreams can come from the carnal realm (soulish, something you ate, medicine you took, and so forth). Dreams can also come from the enemy (deceptive dreams, nightmares, and so forth). Or dreams can come from the Lord. As you practice your skills in deciphering dreams, you may want to refer back to chapter 3 to remind yourself of the basic principles and how God moves through dreams.

Pray Through the Dream

Once you've judged the dream to be accurate, it's time to exercise good stewardship by praying through the dream. But what does it mean to pray through a dream? Take out the journal in which you wrote down the dream. Read through the dream. Although you already may have interpreted large parts of your dream, as you read and pray it's possible to get more revelation on what the Lord said or how to apply it to your life. Praying through the dream is the primary way to unlock deeper meanings.

Consider Your Emotions

In my death dream example, I was shaken. I was so shaken in the dream that I woke up shaken, and it continued to disturb me until I prayed through to peace. In a dream you may feel all sorts of emotions. Sometimes you wake up feeling those same emotions. I've been angry in dreams and woken up angry. I've been joyful in dreams and woken up joyful.

Your emotions will provide major clues about the meanings—and this is also subjective. Skydiving in a dream may make one person feel alive but scare another person terribly. You will not feel strong emotions in every dream you have, so pay close attention when you do. It's a point of reference for God to show you something that you need to face emotionally.

Review the Context

I've said this repeatedly but I want to give a fuller explanation here. *Context* means "the parts of a discourse that surround a word or passage and can throw light on its meaning" and "the interrelated conditions in which something exists or occurs; environment; setting," according to *Merriam-Webster*'s dictionary.

Look for the Lord's Broad Brush

Every detail in a dream has some significance. God doesn't do anything without a purpose. Especially in longer dreams, however, we can get so bogged down in the details we miss the picture the Lord painted for us with a broad brush. Look at the big picture. Is the Lord saying something about your career, your family, your heart? What is the general theme of the dream? Once you have identified the overarching message, interpreting the details will be easier and not so confusing.

Ask Questions

- What is the *main focus* of the dream? Most of your dreams will be about you.
- Were you an observer in your dream? Many times, that indicates a warning dream or a call to intercession.
- Who were the people in your dream and what do they represent?
- What were the names of the people in your dreams?
- Where did the dream take place? What was the setting?
- What was the time period of the dream? Was this in your

past? Was it in a past era? Is the dream pointing to the
future?

- What were the key actions in the dream?
- What colors or numbers stood out?
- What key symbols stood out?
- What was said in the dream? Pay attention to the dialogue
  to discern messages.

Asking the *who, what, when, where,* and *how* can answer a lot
of your *whys* as you pray through the dream.

Dive into the Details

It's been said, the devil is in the details. But I'm here to tell
you *God* is in the details. Explore every facet of the dream you can
remember. Sometimes small details completely change a dream's
meaning. Details can be vital, from colors of shirts to names on
street signs to the weather outside and more. When you seek help
from someone in interpreting the dream, remember to share the
details.

Search for Scripture Parallels

Sometimes dreams will parallel scriptural truths, such as fighting a giant or crossing a river or facing a mountain. If you dream
of mountains, look up what the Bible has to say about mountains.
Let the Bible help you translate your dreams. Although there may
be many different applications of mountains in Scripture, as you
study the Word of God He will often emphasize or highlight the
verses in the context of what He is saying. When you get to the
right Scripture, He'll make sure you know it. Clarity and understanding will come.

Contemplate Multiple Interpretations

Understand that the dream may have different levels of interpretation. God could be saying one thing to you but as you share your dream with someone else who was in your dream, they might see something that you didn't because, yes, God can even speak to others through a dream He gives to you. The dream also could mean one thing now, but more revelation could unfold that would be helpful in your future. This is another reason you should record your dreams.

Find an Interpreter

If a dream is troublesome or you feel strongly that there is a deeper meaning you can't unlock, pray about submitting it to someone who can help you discover what God is saying—and be willing to pray about what they share to judge their interpretation. Not everyone has the gift of interpreting dreams, but sometimes God will show the leaders under whom we serve what He is saying because they are stewards of your soul. Hebrews 13:17 NKJV says, "Obey those who rule over you, and be submissive, for they watch out for your souls, as those who must give account. Let them do so with joy and not with grief, for that would be unprofitable for you."

The Interpretation Belongs to the Lord

Before setting out to interpret the dreams of the butler and the baker from Pharaoh's house, Joseph said, "Do not interpretations belong to God?" (Gen. 40:8 NKJV). *Gill's Exposition of the Entire Bible* offers more insight into this: "For as dreams themselves, which are of importance, and predict things to come, are of God; for none can foretell future events but he, and such to whom he imparts the gift of prophecy; so none can interpret dreams with any certainty but God himself, and those to whom he gives the faculty of interpretation of them."

We need to work with the Spirit of God to unlock interpretations. "For the Spirit searches all things, yes, the deep things of God. For what man knows the things of a man except the spirit of the man which is in him? Even so no one knows the things of God except the Spirit of God" (1 Cor. 2:10–11). "But the natural man does not receive the things of the Spirit of God, for they are foolishness to him; nor can he know them, because they are spiritually discerned" (1 Cor. 2:14 NKJV). Our natural minds can be helpful in assimilating dreams for interpretation but ultimately the accurate interpretation is informed by the God who gave you the dream.

Common Dream Meanings

I can't stress enough how subjective dreams are—how God speaks to you in terms you'll understand and in the context of your life situations much of the time. Still, just as there are biblical dream codes and cultural dream codes and categories of dreams, there are also dreams that are fairly common to man. In other words, there are some dream themes that are consistent to all, if not most, people. We'll explore some of those common dreams in this section.

Bathrooms

Bathrooms represent cleansing. Bathrooms contain toilets, tubs, and showers. God could be delivering or cleansing you from something from your past or in your present. God could be flushing painful wounds or showering you with His love.

Houses

A house could represent your soul, your church, or your home. Pay attention to the rooms you are in, the décor, the lighting, and the other people in the house.

Schools

If you find yourself in school—especially if you are not currently in school—perhaps it represents a season of learning or training in the spirit. While it could mean returning to school, typically it's a symbol of learning and growing in your life—or the need for growth. Ask God what He is trying to show you.

Storms

Dark storms could represent an enemy attack. Sun showers could represent God's blessing. Again, context and emotion matters.

Being Chased

The enemy may be trying to instill fear in your heart so you will run away from an opportunity, a difficult situation, or even spiritual warfare. It could also reveal that something in you—from condemnation to fear of surrendering your whole heart—is causing you to run from God. Ask God what the root issue is if you don't know.

Appearing Naked in Public

This could be good or bad. On the good side, appearing naked in public could represent your willingness or need to be transparent. On the bad side, it could mean that you feel vulnerable. Ask God to show you what you need to understand about yourself.

Pregnancy and Babies

Pregnancy and babies represent birthing something new. It could mean birthing a relationship or a job or a ministry. It could represent a witty invention, a new anointing, a new friend, or a new season in your life.

Losing Teeth

Losing teeth can point to stress, loss, or confusion in your life. Consider what we do with our teeth. We chew things. God could be speaking to you about a loss of something important or a lack of wisdom (wisdom teeth being pulled) or discernment (eye teeth falling out). Ask God to give you wisdom and discernment.

Losing Your Wallet or Purse

Dreams in which you lose your wallet or purse deal with a sense of loss or searching for identity or purpose. They can also signify an attack by the enemy on who you are in Christ, your authority, or your destiny.

Missing or Arriving Late for an Appointment

If you dream you are missing appointments, missing trains, missing planes, or showing up late for parties, and so forth, it could be a warning that you are about to miss something God has planned for you. This is a wake-up call to be more spiritually alert and readily prepared. Ask God to help you ready yourself and correctly discern the season.

Falling

Different from flying, falling dreams represent a fear of losing control or being out of control. This could be a soulish dream based on anxiety, or God showing you that you need to cultivate more self-discipline over your life or that you need to give Him control. Ask God to help you cultivate self-discipline and repent if you've tried to control what you should be giving to God.

Flying

Flying dreams are typically good dreams. They often indicate you are soaring in the spirit, rising above difficulties in life, attaining God's perspective, and experiencing new levels of freedom or spiritual growth. A fear of flying in a dream could mean you are scared about going to the next level with God, in a relationship, or in your career.

Dead Friends or Relatives

We've talked about the significance of death in a dream in previous chapters. It could mean death of a person, but death is usually symbolic of a relationship or season in your life. What could it mean when you see dead friends or family members in dreams? God may be showing you there are generational curses in your blood line. It could also be a familiar spirit speaking to you in your dream. A familiar spirit appears friendly, maybe even as a friend or a family member, but it's a demon in disguise. Ask the Lord to show you and help you be discerning. Proceed with caution.

Transportation

Transportation in dreams—from cars to trains to boats to planes—can represent your career or ministry. You're going places. Consider the mode of transportation. You can go faster and carry more people with you in an airplane than you can a bicycle. For example, the dreamer in an airplane may be rising in influence.

Common Dream Interpretation Pitfalls

There's both an art and science to decoding your dreams. It gets easier with practice in terms of the mechanics of understanding symbols and numbers. But there are always pitfalls, usually when we get ahead of God, behind God, or in the way of God. Let's look at a few of the most common dream deciphering pitfalls.

Sharing Your Dream with the Wrong People

Sharing your dream and its interpretation with the wrong people can cause a setback in the interpretation or even in your life. In the Sermon on the Mount, Jesus said, "Do not give what is holy to the dogs; nor cast your pearls before swine, lest they trample them under their feet, and turn and tear you in pieces" (Matt. 7:6 NKJV). Jesus wasn't calling men dogs or swine—He was talking about attitudes of the heart. Many people do not have the mind of Christ with regard to dreams. They may discount dreams or your dreams may even offend them, as was the case with Joseph and his eleven brothers.

Joseph had two dreams. In the first dream, one sheaf of wheat stood up straight while eleven sheaves bowed down to it. In the second dream, the son, the moon, and the stars bowed down to Joseph (Gen. 37:1–10). Joseph's father rebuked him and his brothers wanted to kill him but instead sold him into slavery. While Joseph's prophetic dream manifested many years later, this example demonstrates the need to be careful not to tell everything we hear to everybody. With regard to the prophetic words spoken over Jesus being the Messiah, "Mary kept all these things and pondered them in her heart" (Luke 2:19 NKJV). She didn't blow trumpets and make announcements to glorify herself or her son for the sake of recognition.

Taking Everything Literally

Dreams can have very literal aspects, but one of the biggest mistakes we make in our dream interpretations is to take literally what God is using as symbolic or parabolic. I've mentioned, for example, that a person in a dream could be a person in your life but just as often is *symbolic* of something in your life. If you see a person in your dream, don't automatically assume it's really that person. Consider what they represent in your life. This is also subjective. In a dream, Hitler to a German might represent something very different from what he would represent to a Jewish person. As in my opening dream interpretation, death didn't mean literal death—but there could be times when the Lord would show you a literal death in a dream.

Getting Hung Up on What You Don't Understand

As in my dream interpretation at the beginning of this chapter, there are some parts of the dream that you may not understand. God may be hiding some revelation until a later time. You can continue to ponder and pray about it, but don't let it hang up the rest of your quest for a meaning. If something you don't understand is pivotal to the interpretation, God will make it clear as you seek His heart.

Let this Scripture guide you: "Test all things; hold fast what is good" (1 Thess. 5:21–23 NKJV). Remember, it's possible that some dreams are not from God, so you need to test or judge them and hold fast to what's good. You may have several dreams in one night, some of which are from God and others that are not.

Making One Symbol Fit Everything

By now I'm sure you understand that one symbol does not fit all. For example, a dog in a dream could mean one thing to you and another thing to someone else. There are experiential and cultural elements involved in dream interpretation that we must strongly consider. You have a unique dream language, though the Word of God can be of tremendous value in interpretation.

Acting on a Dream Before Getting Confirmation

We need to seek prophetic confirmation. The simple gift of prophecy can often be confirmed with Scripture. But directional words should be confirmed if they are going to change the course of a life or ministry. "This is the third time I am coming to you. In the mouth of two or three witnesses shall every word be established" (2 Cor. 13:1 KJV).

Interpreting Others' Dreams Through Your Dream Language

Remember, dream codes are subjective to each person. What a dream may mean to you could carry a totally different meaning for another person.

Chapter 9

EXAMPLES OF DREAMS AND INTERPRETATIONS

Now that you are armed with the basics of interpreting dreams, it's time to put that knowledge to good use. It's time to see how we apply those spiritual skills to work. I will share dreams from my life to demonstrate firsthand how I navigated the process of dream interpretation.

As you read through these pages, by the Spirit of God you may see things I never saw. You'll certainly see how a dream interpretation book would have given me, at times, only part of the message God was trying to send—or even a wrong answer altogether.

I am intentionally pointing out in these dream interpretations how I came to these conclusions, how my soul tried to trick me, how people and dream interpretation books would have led me in a wrong direction, and how subjective dream interpretation really is.

Dream: The Messy Apartment

I dreamed I was in a very messy apartment. It was not the condo I was currently living in, and I didn't see any other room except the living room, if you could call it that. The living room was unlivable. It was covered wall to wall with furniture and boxes. It was as if things were being randomly stored everywhere—or as if things were boxed up in preparation of moving out, except I was living there.

In the dream, I was intentional about the order in which I did each thing. I started by getting rid of everything that did not belong there. I left nothing untouched. I started pulling furniture away from the walls. I noticed the sideboard cabinet was facing the wrong way—the drawers were facing the wall so they could not be opened. I pulled the cabinet away from the wall and turned it around the right way so I could open and close the doors and drawers. As I started rearranging the furniture, I noticed how much dirt there was.

I removed everything that did not belong and cleaned up all the dirt. I removed rubbish from the living room and put it into oversized trash bags. Next, I assessed the room so I could strategically rearrange what was left, hoping it would fit together better.

At that point, a man who looked like my ex-husband came into the living room. He liked what I was doing but did not do anything to help. He just watched me as I worked. When I asked him why he hadn't called me, he said he was over his minutes on his cell phone plan. I asked him how that was possible, since we were on an unlimited family plan. He said he had changed to another carrier.

Interpretation

This dream is rich in symbology—both objective and subjective. Let's look at the breakdown of this dream and how I worked with the Spirit of God to draw certain conclusions that helped bring confirmation in a season of transition.

Again, dream languages are personal. Some things, though, are fairly set. I'll start out with a broad brush on this interpretation, then we'll drill down into details. In the dream, I was in my house, and it was out of order. This was not someone else's house. It was my house—even though it did not look like any house I've ever lived in. I knew in the dream it was my house.

The house was out of order, and I was putting it in order. Was this my house or did it symbolize something else? A house often represents a church, and in this case the house was the Awakening House of Prayer.

Let's look at the next clue: the living room. A living room is a public space in a house. If this had been my bedroom, this dream could have been pointing to an issue in my heart. If it had been a bathroom, it could have been dealing with an issue in my soul that needed cleansing—or a mind-set that needed to be washed with the water of the Word. But this was the *living room*. Since a house can represent a church, and a living room is a public place, we can draw the conclusion—informed by the Spirit of God—that this was my church.

Furniture can represent an old agreement with people or unresolved issues. At Awakening House of Prayer, I had made an arrangement in the past with some people in the ministry, but some had unresolved issues in their hearts that prevented them from keeping their part of the agreement. The Lord gave me another dream during this same time period about lockers in the lobby of a church, which represented issues hidden in the heart. I had given positions of authority to some members of the church, but they were not living up to the responsibilities that came with that authority. They wanted to but were not able.

Sometimes a backward object in a dream can signify something being unprepared or unable to move forward. Again, the people in positions of authority in the dream were not prepared—they were not able—to move forward with the vision God gave me. The rubbish in the living room speaks to getting rid of things that are no longer helpful or useful—or things that are getting in the way. Rubbish can also symbolize dead works that need to be removed.

What does this have to do with my ex-husband? Remember, people in your dream don't always represent the people in real life—but a person may represent something specifically to you. For me, my ex-husband represents betrayal by someone I was in close covenant with. The Lord was trying to show me someone in my house—in my church—with whom I was in close relationship, was going to betray me through the process of putting things in order. It was a warning from the Lord to prepare my heart.

Let's look at the telephone issues. Telephones are used to communicate. In the dream, I asked my ex-husband why he hadn't called me. I was expecting to hear from him—I was expecting his help in the transition. He indicated he had used all his minutes. I was trying to get to the root of the communication problem.

As part of the interpretation, keep in mind that the problem was not with *my* phone but with *his* phone. The communication issue was not on my end; the communication issue was on his end. He chose to come out of the family plan—to come out of unity with me—and sign up for a plan that restricted communication without even bothering to tell me. This reveals magnified communication problems. That decision was costly: he went over minutes, and I had to personally pay for that because the billing was in my name. This indicates I was to pay a price for someone else's lack of communication and decision to come out of unity without any discussion or warning.

My ex-husband also changed carriers. This was an act of divorce. This was an act of self-will. Now, the specific carrier part of the dream is especially subjective to me. I view that carrier as inferior because I had tremendous issues with the company's reception, as well as billing issues. My personal experience with the carrier hinders communication and wastes my money. I would never choose to work with this company again because it let me down so many times.

In the dream, I saw my ex-husband transitioning to the new carrier as a poor decision. In the natural, some people in the ministry were consistently making poor decisions in addition to the failure to communicate. Looking up the meaning of the word *sprint* was also part of this dream interpretation. *Sprint* means to run at full speed—but only for a short distance. We need endurance. Operating a church is not a marathon. We need a steadfast spirit, not an up and down, double-minded soul. The good news is I took authority over all this and put the house (the church) in order.

Context also matters here. At the time of this dream, I was struggling with feelings of wanting to give up on the house of prayer because of all the problems. I could not seem to get everyone on the same page. Soon after the dream—and encouraged by the dream—I started setting the house in order. I hired two campus pastors to help carry the load, moved people out of positions who were unwilling or unprepared to move forward, and, in other words, cleaned house. One person would betray me in the process. The dream manifested in a very short time period. Most of my dreams do. All dreams don't.

Dream: A Friend Presses Me to Move into Her House

In one of the most significant warning dreams I've ever had, the Lord revealed that a person I was walking with was a dangerous alignment. These sorts of dreams are difficult to process because you want to believe the best of people, but sometimes issues run deep and the enemy can use them to tear down what God is trying to build in your life.

I had a dream I was in this particular woman's house. I will call her Betty. Betty was trying to convince me to move into her house. She was making a hard sell, citing the benefits and why it made so much sense. I was listening to her but was not swayed—not in the least. Actually, her insistence was frustrating.

In the dream but not in the natural, Betty's house was in a city named Pompano Beach, about a forty-five-minute drive north and inconvenient to everything going on in my life. There was no perspective from which it made any sense—or why she would think it made any sense—for me to leave my debt-free home on the beach and move into her small condo. While I was in Betty's house, I watched a small fire begin in the kitchen. I said, "Betty, there's a fire in your house."

She said, "Oh, that's nothing. Don't worry about that."

Then it erupted into a bigger fire, though it was contained in the kitchen sink. The fire was clearly dangerous. She downplayed the fire and continued trying to get me to agree to move into her house. I said no, in no uncertain terms.

An elder Asian man who was showing me the property wanted to show me the parking garage below the condo. I went down and saw three parking spots with three green and white vehicles. One was a sedan, the other a smaller vehicle, and the third one was a low-to-the-ground adult tricycle.

The Asian man indicated I would have access to these vehicles if I moved in with Betty. He insisted I take the tricycle for a spin but warned me to watch out for the cat. There was a cat roaming in the garage, he said, with extremely long and sharp claws. This cat, he explained, would pounce on people and cause severe injuries. After much cajoling, I finally got on the tricycle and tried to ride it but was not able to. I could not navigate it. It was awkward. I had to work to avoid the cat pouncing on me while I was in the garage. I got off the tricycle and left.

Interpretation

Here's the interpretation: In this case, Betty was really Betty. Betty was not symbolic of anything or anyone. Her real name is not important in this dream as there was no symbolism or insight that came with her real name.

My dream exposed Betty's hidden agenda: She wanted me to do things her way. She wanted me to move into her house. Ultimately, she wanted me to do church her way. In the natural Betty was a seasoned minister and came into my church when it was small. She had ideas to grow the congregation, but none of them bore witness with me, so I never agreed to execute the ideas. She persisted under the guise of "sharing wisdom."

Now let's look at the different elements of the dream. Fire can be positive or negative. In this context, fire was not a good thing. On the negative side, fire can represent strife, anger, gossip, jealousy, or even hell. The fire was in her kitchen. A kitchen is symbolic of many things, according to dream interpretation books. It could mean preparation, as we prepare meals in the kitchen. It could mean the church, indicating something under pressure or even the human spirit. In this case, it meant none of those things. This is a good example of why dream interpretation books aren't always helpful in the final interpretation. The interpretation belongs to God (Gen. 40:8).

When I warned Betty about the fire—a growing fire—in her kitchen, she downplayed it. She would not deal with it. She tried to convince me it was nothing. The fire continued burning the entire time I was in her house. As it turns out, this was a fire of strife that I would soon see manifest in the natural. The Lord was warning me there was strife in her heart. The Bible says where strife exists, you'll also find confusion and every evil thing (James 3:16).

In the dream, the garage scene held a strategic key to the interpretation. What do you do in a garage? In a positive context, a garage protects from the weather but, generally speaking, garages deal with storage. When a car—which can symbolize a ministry or career—is in a garage, it's not going anywhere. In some instances, when a car is in a garage it's because it's broken down, needs a tune up, an oil change, a new tire, or some other repair. When cars are in a garage, they are parked. They are removed from operation. Are you getting the picture?

Before we further interpret the garage, let's take a look at what was going on in the garage. There were three vehicles painted green and white. While green could speak to health or prosperity, in this context it speaks of jealousy and envy and wicked works. Like the fire, this was another confirmation of strife in Betty's heart. There were three vehicles in the garage. The Lord showed me Betty started out with bigger cars, but at this stage in her life—she was an older woman—she was riding the tricycle. The Asian man wanted me to ride the tricycle. A tricycle is a lower form of transportation than a bicycle.

In the dream world, transportation is important and offers clues to a dream's meaning. If you start off on a jetliner in one dream and then a year later end up on a motor bike, something is wrong. You're not moving ahead—you are moving backward. The Asian man wanted me to come into agreement with Betty's ideas—Betty's ways of doing church, which were influenced by envy and strife. He wanted me to ride the tricycle. In the dream, I got on the tricycle but quickly got off. It was not suitable for me.

Cats often represent evil or witchcraft. Cats can also represent rebellion or vicious attacks. In this context, since the Asian man warned me about the cat's propensity to attack, the Lord was showing me Betty represented a vicious attack against my ministry and any alignment with her—any agreement with her ways—would leave me in a garage riding a tricycle, spiritually speaking. Betty was carrying a foul spirit.

One final point of interpretation is the name of the city Betty lived in. Pompano. Betty was trying to get me to move out of my territory—out of my assignment. She wanted me to move to Pompano—which means "clam." Clams spend most of their lives partially buried in the sand of the ocean floor. If I did not cut off this toxic relationship, the spiritual attack would leave me buried, hidden.

I cut off this relationship in a responsible and healthy way, never revealing the dream to her but clearly standing against the spirit influencing Betty. We are still friends, but we do not walk together.

Dream: The Golden Gate Bridge

In this dream I was on a journey, and it was time to move on to the next phase of the trip. I was waiting on Michelle, but it was taking her so long I decided to move on without her. I was driving a car, and I pulled up to the edge of a huge bridge. I looked up and recognized the Golden Gate Bridge. I was a little nervous and intimidated. I thought, *Wow, that's a big bridge!* Ultimately, I did not drive across the bridge because I decided I could not go forward without Michelle. I backed up the car and waited.

Interpretation

This was a dream related to my personal ministry. The name of this bridge is significant. Golden can signify the glory of God, purity, and holiness. A gate is essentially a door or can represent opportunity. A bridge represents transition.

Michelle was a real person in my life. In this dream, I wasn't waiting on Michelle—someone who used to walk closely with me but who had moved to another city. In this dream, I had to examine what Michelle represents to me in order to understand what the Lord was saying.

Michelle represents to me intercession and natural administrative help, as well as godly counsel. She was my first full-time intercessor and also booked my travel and arranged many other things in the ministry. In the dream, I decided I did not have the support to move ahead in what God had called me to do, so I backed up. The Lord was showing me a hesitancy in my heart to move forward without the right support. This dream confirmed this was the Lord's wisdom.

Dream: Prosperity in the Coffee Shop

This next dream is simple and yet profound. In the dream I was on a journey with my mother and father. We stopped to rest. I wanted to get some coffee, but I had no money. My mother gave me a one-dollar, a ten-dollar, and a one-hundred-dollar bill.

I walked over to the coffee shop next door and ordered coffee while they waited. The coffee was served in a large, round goblet, topped with super-creamy milk and honey drizzled on top. I thought, *Wow, I've never seen this kind of coffee before!* It was so good!

I approached the barista to pay for the coffee. She told me it was eight dollars and some change. I thought, *I don't want to break the one-hundred-dollar bill; I'll pay with the ten-dollar bill.* The barista gave me back way more money than I gave her. I told her she had made a mistake, but she insisted I was supposed to have the money.

Interpretation

My mother and father in the dream were not actually my mother and father. Although the Holy Spirit is not a woman, sometimes in the dream world a motherly figure can represent the Holy Spirit, who is the most nurturing and comforting member of the

Godhead. My mother and father in this dream represent the Holy Spirit and Father God. How exciting to be on a journey with God!

This dream is also interesting because it involves numbers. In the Bible, the number one typically represents God or unity. The number ten signifies completion. The number one hundred stands for maximum blessing. In Jesus' explanation of the parable of the sower, He said some of the seed "produce a hundredfold, some sixty, some thirty" (Matt. 13:23). Can God be limited? When Jesus said the seed produced a hundredfold return, He was talking about a maximum blessing. God was not *limiting* our sowing to a hundredfold return.

Here's where we need to be subjective. When I wake up at four o'clock in the morning to pray and read the Word, I brew a cup of coffee. For me, coffee symbolizes my time spent fellowshipping with the Holy Spirit and also time spent fellowshipping with my close friends. Some credible Christian dream interpretation books, like *The Divinity Code*, list fellowshipping with the Holy Spirit as one possible meaning of coffee. In Scripture, milk and honey symbolize provision, plenty, and fulfilled promises—or entering into the promised land.

In this dream, the Lord was showing me He had provision planned for me. This was a prophetic dream showing things to come. I was already walking in provision, but the Lord was calling me to go on a journey with Him and enter into full-time ministry. Although I'd been in ministry for fifteen years at that point, I was not in full-time ministry. I was bi-vocational.

God was preparing my heart to trust Him for provision when I followed Him out of the world and into the promised land that I couldn't even see yet. When the time came to take the leap of faith into full-time ministry, the Holy Spirit put me in remembrance of this dream and it encouraged my heart.

Dream: NBA MVP LeBron James Gives Me Advice

Remember how a particular person in a dream can symbolize something? A great example is my dream in which LeBron James offered me advice. In the dream, I walked into a women's basketball training facility. Activity was buzzing. It was a bright facility and people were hard at work training. As I walked down the halls observing everything, I noticed LeBron, who was there to coach and inspire the women. I walked up to him and described a problem I was having with a young woman in training. He told me he agreed with me that she would make it through and would not be cut from the team. That was the extent of the dream. It was short and concise, but packed with meaning.

Interpretation

The interpretation is partly subjective because the context of this dream was particular to my ministry. A certain young woman was highly gifted in the spiritual realm, very prophetic, but also very critical. She was in training under my leadership but had been offended by some loving correction. I was personally coaching her at the time I met with LeBron in my dream.

This may bother you, but remember dreams are subjective and symbolic. LeBron in this dream was not a VIP basketball player—but he did symbolize a Very Important Person. LeBron symbolized

Jesus. Consider LeBron's nickname: the King. Who is the King? Jesus Christ is the King of kings and the Lord of lords. In this dream, LeBron symbolized Jesus expressing His will for this young woman to make it through and for me to continue coaching her.

The training facility represented my ministry, in which many people would be trained. Remember, this was a sports facility. Sports in the dream world carries a spiritual warfare connotation—and there was certainly spiritual warfare over this young woman's destiny. For weeks my entire team was in intercession for her. Jesus is the Chief Intercessor and He was in agreement with our efforts to keep praying for her.

This dream fueled our intercession. It gave us faith that this young woman wasn't yet a lost cause. The enemy was trying to take her out, but we were standing in the gap.

Chapter 10

APPLICATION OF
DREAM REVELATIONS

We know that God does not waste anything. The study of dreams must include how to apply what we learn from our dreams, how God is trying to lead us. The best illustrations I can offer come from my own experience.

We were planning a big conference and I was tasked with looking for a church that would host the event. I immediately thought of an influential pastor who had a sizable facility. I knew him personally, so I reached out without giving it any real thought. As it turned out, he had always wanted to meet one of the key speakers on the conference agenda. The pastor told me he would try to work out the dates and get back to me.

That same night, I had a disturbing dream. I was in my bedroom getting dressed to go out. I saw this influential pastor in my bed, fully clothed but nevertheless in my bed. He patted on the spot next to him and said, "Come over here and sit down so we can talk about the event." The thought made me uncomfortable, so I went and sat on the very edge of the bed. Then he tried to seduce me.

When I woke up, I was shocked and grieved. The Lord was clearly showing me there was a seducing spirit operating in this influential pastor's meeting. This was a warning dream. I shared it with one of the elder conference organizers and he told me that we would not be holding the conference at that church.

This very short dream revealed the motives of this pastor and the spirit he was operating in. With the Holy Spirit's help, we were able to immediately apply the revelation to our situation and avoid a potential entanglement with someone we didn't need to work with.

Of course, not all dreams are so straightforward in their interpretations or applications. But many are, if we'll examine the context—our life situations, decisions we're trying to make, and people we're involved with.

After you've decoded your dreams—gaining as much enlightenment as you can in the present—take care and use wisdom to apply the revelations to your circumstances. Much like a prophetic word, you can receive an accurate word and interpretation but it is important for you to take faith-inspired action to apply what God is showing you.

Keep in mind that God may be showing you something for the future; therefore the application may be partial for now and then will be fully completed later. How do you determine if the dream is for now, later, or both? God, who gave you the dream, will help you see what you need to do now and what you need to do in the future if you ask Him. He's not in the business of hiding His wisdom from you. James 1:5 NKJV assures us that "if any of you lacks wisdom, let him ask of God, who gives to all liberally and without reproach, and it will be given to him."

When you receive a dream, you have to consider if it's conditional or a sovereign decree of God's. Is He showing you something that has already happened and is providing insight, something that is happening now that you need to take action on, or something that will happen in the future that you can prevent or need to come into agreement with?

Most personal prophecy is conditional, requiring faith and works on our part to receive it. God's sovereign decrees—such as messianic and end-times prophecies—will come to pass. Much the same, revelations you receive in a dream can be like signs on the highway to destiny. They point you in the right direction, but you have to walk down the path, and fight the good fight of faith along with plenty of demons to get to the finish line. Warning dreams often demand immediate action.

The challenge with applying the revelation you receive in dreams is often the timetable. God rarely moves as fast as we'd like Him to, but sometimes we don't move as quickly as we need to. Recurring dreams that become more repetitive signal an urgency in the heart of God that time is drawing near to act, or that you should have acted already.

By contrast, if we get ahead of God, we make a mess. This is what Joseph did in telling his brothers the dreams he had about the family bowing down to him (Gen. 37:5–11).

Joseph didn't understand the depths of what he was dreaming or he probably would not have shared it. He was young. He was intrigued. His brothers interpreted the dreams and in their jealousy and insecurity decided to apply the dream for Joseph by throwing him into a pit and selling him as a slave to avoid the dream manifesting. Consider the following scene:

> Now when they saw him afar off, even before he came near them, they conspired against him to kill him. Then they said to one another, "Look, this dreamer is coming! Come therefore, let us now kill him and cast him into some pit; and we shall say, 'Some wild beast has devoured him.' We shall see what will become of his dreams!" (Gen. 37:18–20 NKJV)

Reuben had enough sense to stop the killing, but ultimately they sold Joseph for twenty sheckles of silver and he ended up in Egypt. It's doubtful Joseph understood his dream until Pharaoh had the dream of seven years of plenty and seven years of famine. At that point, Joseph began connecting the dots, seeking wisdom from God for a strategy to save the world, and was exalted in the natural just as he was in the dream.

As you can see, there are times when the application of a dream may be far into the future. The response when we don't know how to apply a dream should be to watch and pray—and wait.

Forcing Dreams into Reality

When applying a revelation you receive in dreams—especially prophetic dreams—be careful not to try to "help" them come to pass. Adding works to your faith is one thing; trying to manipulate a situation to see a prophecy manifest is another.

Abram had a prophecy direct from the mouth of God that he would be the father to many nations. As she was barren, Sarai encouraged Abram to take a shortcut by sleeping with another woman to bring an heir into the world. Abram went into Sarai's maid, Hagar, who birthed Ishmael. God changed Abram's name to Abraham and Sarai's name to Sarah. God in His grace still gave Sarah and Abraham their own son—Isaac—but there was trouble in their house for years because they tried to make a prophetic word come to pass without waiting on God.

With regard to applying the revelation we receive in dreams, remember there's a process to get to the promise. David waited more than twenty years between his anointing in front of his brothers and his kingship. The process doesn't always take that long, but we must cooperate and be patient with the grace of God despite our frustrations and weariness.

Personal prophecies are conditional promises and so are some revelations we receive in dreams. The Bible says to imitate those "who through faith and patience inherit the promises" (Heb. 6:12 NKJV). Remember, "the Lord is not slow concerning His promise, as some count slowness" (2 Peter 3:9).

Progressive Dream Applications

If you've kept record of your dreams over the years, you've probably noticed that at least some of the revelations played out a little differently—or maybe a lot differently—than you expected. You also may be experiencing what I call the "progressive application" of your prophetic revelation.

When you received revelation in a dream, you applied it to your life or ministry in the best way you knew how at the time. That application wasn't wrong, but it may not have been the fullness of God's prophetic intent. Often, it takes years for a dream to realize its full manifestation, as we saw in the life of Joseph. The good news is you can take steps toward the manifestation as more particulars of the dream revelation unfold through prayer and what I call "aha moments" with God, those moments when things suddenly click, as with Joseph's dreams.

I've experienced this a number of times in the last decade. You could view it as God connecting the dots of your prophetic destiny, but it runs deeper than that. When you experience progressive application of a prophetic revelation, you're essentially growing into the dream. At first you didn't have the capacity to walk in the completeness of what the Lord was showing you, so you entered into a training ground that allowed you to apply the principles of the prophetic word on a smaller scale.

The Ezra and Ezekiel Revelations

One of the best examples I can offer from my personal life is what I now affectionately refer to as the "Ezra revelation." In Ezra 4 we discover that the work on the house of God in Jerusalem ceased after much resistance and opposition. After some time, the restoration of the temple resumed with prophets playing a key role.

> Then the prophet Haggai and Zechariah the son of Iddo, prophets, prophesied to the Jews who were in Judah and Jerusalem, in the name of the God of Israel, who was over them. So Zerubbabel the son of Shealtiel and Jeshua the son of Jozadak rose up and began to build the house of God which is in Jerusalem; and the prophets of God were with them, helping them. (Ezra 5:1–2 NKJV)

When I saw this Scripture, the Lord spoke to my heart about the role of prophetic ministry in building—or rebuilding, as it were—God's house. I was convinced the application was a weekly meeting with the prophets in our congregation during which we would pray and seek the Lord for prophetic strategies about building the local church. That wasn't wrong, but ten years later I believe the prophetic revelation God was pouring into my heart was about more than one local church—it has to do with an awakening in America.

Another strong example of revisiting the application of prophetic words is what I affectionately refer to as the "Ezekiel revelation." I was on a difficult missions trip in Latin America when the Lord directed me to Ezekiel 3 and then to Ezekiel 33. In Ezekiel 3 God calls Ezekiel to be a watchman and gives him a mandate:

> "Son of man, I have made you a watchman for the house of Israel; therefore hear a word from My mouth, and give them warning from Me: When I say to the wicked, 'You shall surely die,' and you give him no warning, nor speak to warn the wicked from his wicked way, to save his life, that same wicked man shall die in his iniquity; but his blood I will require at your hand. Yet, if you warn the wicked, and he does not turn from his wickedness, nor from his wicked way, he shall die in his iniquity; but you have delivered your soul." (Ezek. 3:17–19 NKJV)

A similar command is found in Ezekiel 33:7–9. When I read these verses, the fear of the Lord struck my heart. I knew that I needed to be faithful to step out and share the prophetic warnings I was receiving during that season of my ministry, even though nobody really wanted to hear them. I had no understanding at the time that I would pen a "Watchman on the Wall" column that would sound the alarm in the nations of the world.

Warning Dreams (in War)

Many times, warning dreams—or intercessory prayer dreams—will lead you into warfare. In other words, sometimes applying the revelation you received in a dream requires you to go on the offensive before the enemy backs you into a corner. In warning dreams God is giving you a heads-up of danger, essentially providing a way of escape before you need it. In intercessory prayer dreams, God is showing you something to encourage you to stand in the gap and prevent the negative outcome the enemy has planned or to usher in a glorious blessing God has in mind.

I have had many warning dreams that have sent me into warfare. In one dream I was in a car with someone else driving. It wasn't a taxi, but I got into the car thinking I was heading somewhere I asked to go. In fact, I was on the road I usually take to the airport. Soon I realized it was taking too long to get to the airport, and the road became unfamiliar. We had left the well-traveled road, and there were no streetlights to penetrate the darkness. I could not discern where we were.

When I asked the driver where we were, he said we needed to stop at a shop and not to worry. When we went inside, it was clear to me I was in danger. It was a strange backwoods shop like you'd see in horror movies in which people are killed. I had my phone with me, but it only had 37 percent battery.

I walked behind a display shelf while the driver was discussing something with the shop owner. Out of their eyesight, I began trying to text one of my intercessors to let her know something was wrong, but the letters kept coming out skewed and illegible. Something was scrambling the communication. I was finally able to type out a message alerting my intercessor I was in danger and suggesting she track my phone. When I emerged from behind the shelf, the driver and shop owner kept insisting they were protecting me. I told them I would be missed, and they said they had arranged everything so no one would be concerned.

Interpretation

In the dream I was kidnapped. To *kidnap* means "to seize and detain or carry away by unlawful force or fraud and often with demand for ransom." It was interesting that this was a stealth kidnapping. There was no force in the initial taking. It was a kidnapping by deception. I ordered a driver and the enemy showed up.

A dark road denotes some manner of wickedness. What about the number thirty-seven? When decoding numbers like this, you typically have to break them apart, so we can look at three and seven or thirty and seven. The number thirty denotes divine order or good timing, and seven represents divine order or perfection. Clearly, in the dream everything was in disorder, but my phone showed 37 percent battery on my touchscreen. In the dream, my immediate response was prayer—calling an intercessor to bring divine order into the situation. The enemy tried to interfere with the communication, but I broke through.

Summarizing the dream's interpretation: I was on my way to the airport on a ministry assignment. The enemy hijacked the vehicle and tried to sidetrack me. Although I wasn't in any real danger physically, the enemy was trying to intercept my call. But

I called (texted) anyway. In the natural, this revelation sent all my intercessors into prayer. This danger has not manifested because the Devil's plans were crushed in the spirit by applying the revelation I received in a dream.

Understanding Recurring Dreams

I call them "baby dreams"—and these prophetic encounters have been a running theme in my life during the past decade. It seems God has been laboring with me to birth a new thing for nearly that long. Along the way, there was at least one Ishmael, a couple of near-abortions, and plenty of spiritual warfare. But God in His grace somehow worked all things together for good.

There were lessons in this series of prophetic dreams. When I put those principles into practice it caused what looked like a still-birth to become a healthy baby. I still don't have all the answers, but God has made one thing clear to me: sometimes a small shift makes all the difference.

First Baby Dream: Surrendering My Will

The "baby dreams" started about eight years ago. I had a dream I was pregnant. I was not happy about it because it was going to turn my life upside down—but I knew I couldn't do anything about it. I tried to pretend it wasn't real, but ultimately pretending wasn't an option. The lesson of this first prophetic dream was that I had to be like Mary, who gave her will over to the Lord despite the trouble it was going to cause her in the natural. I woke up and committed in my heart to let the Lord's will be done in my life and moved ahead.

Second Baby Dream: Birthing a Man-Child

About a year after that prophetic encounter, I had a second "baby dream." This time I was in the hospital giving birth. When the baby was born, it was a man-child. It seemed to be a baby, but it had the features of a full-grown man. Immediately after the baby was born, he started running toward his goal. Those around me said, "It must be nice to birth a full-grown ministry. That's what you can expect."

Third Baby Dream: Making Adjustments

Fast-forward another five years. I was in a very uncomfortable position, having the weight of a church plant unexpectedly fall on my shoulders. I didn't sign up to preach, pray, prophesy, and administrate the whole church, but that's what was happening. I was at a crossroads, praying about whether I should exit or continue to bear the weight—and the spiritual warfare—of another man's vision or move on.

I went to sleep and had another "baby dream." This time I was pregnant. I still wasn't thrilled. I was hungry and the only thing available was some strange combination of eggs and pepperoni. My chair was too low for me to comfortably type on my computer. I had to change into clothes I didn't like. I was thinking about how I could possibly hit the gym with all of this going on. I thought about how I'd be sixty before this kid was grown.

In other words, I was doing a lot of natural reasoning. Eventually, I changed my clothes into something that wasn't ideal but wasn't too uncomfortable. I ate the eggs for the protein and skipped the unhealthy pepperoni. I got a taller chair so I could type more comfortably. Then I woke up. I told one of my friends involved in the church plant about the dream, including the eggs and pepperoni. I had never heard of eggs and pepperoni as a dish—but it was one of her favorites. (Go figure. God wanted her to bear witness to the dream.)

From that dream I learned that I had to make sacrifices and adjustments to do the will of God. In other words, there would be some aspects of birthing this ministry that were uncomfortable, but there were ways to adjust to the circumstances and plow through the pain to get to the goal line and God's ultimate will. At first I thought it was a message to keep bearing the weight of the church plant. But when the church planter manifested with wrong motives, it became abundantly clear that his vision wasn't my burden to bear, and God released me. He used the experience to push me into what He really had in mind the whole time.

Fourth Baby Dream: Shifting Your Direction

In the last "baby dream," I finally got the message—and it changed everything. I was nine months pregnant, but the baby had stopped moving. The baby wasn't kicking or rolling or showing any sign of life. This is how I felt after leaving the church plant.

In the prophetic dream I thought the baby was dead and I panicked. Then, suddenly, I had the unction to shift the baby's position with gentle pressure from my hand. I later researched this and discovered there's a name for it: the Diaphragmatic Release Technique. When I did, I could feel the baby kicking again, and I knew all was well.

Here's the lesson I took away from this dream, which connected with the previous baby dreams: sometimes things look dead, but you just have to reposition yourself for life to return. It doesn't always take very much. Just one gentle movement in the right direction can cause God to breathe on that thing again so you can birth it and begin nurturing what God has given you to steward.

When it comes to biblical dream interpretation, there are many principles you'll learn from this book. One you need to understand at the beginning is that there is a *kairos* time for your dream to come to pass. It could be the next day after you have the dream or, like Joseph, twenty years later. The Greek word *kairos* means a fitting season, opportunity, time, or occasion. It comes from the Greek word *kara*, referring to things "coming to a head." Kairos is the suitable time, the right moment, or the favorable moment. There's a right moment to apply the revelation in your divinely inspired dreams. There's a right moment to enter into the prophetic dreams God has revealed to you.

We Know in Part

Here's the lesson—and it's an important one for every believer, whether you move in prophetic ministry, receive personal prophecy in a prayer line, or just hear the still, small voice of God for yourself: "we know in part and we prophesy in part" (1 Cor. 13:9–12 NKJV). "We see through a glass, darkly" (1 Cor. 13:12 KJV). Revelation is progressive, and prophetic words can unfold over time with deeper application.

Record the prophetic words, dreams, and visions you receive, and seek to put the truth within them into practice today. But don't stop there. Continue to refer back to your journals over time, and you may see clearly how the Lord has shifted dynamics to bring you into a deeper application of a prophetic revelation.

Move with the Holy Spirit at the level you are now and always expect Him to take you deeper. Remember, God is able to "do exceedingly abundantly above all that we ask or think, according to the power that worketh in us" (Eph. 3:20 KJV). Instead of limiting the application of your dreams, remain open to new revelations that will take you deeper into His will.

Chapter 11

STRATEGICALLY STEWARDING YOUR DREAM LIFE

S tewardship. It's a word we often associate with our finances. God wants us to be a good steward—a fancy word for manager or supervisor—of our finances, but that's certainly not where stewardship ends. Stewardship is a running theme through everything the Lord gives us.

Peter wrote about stewarding the gifts of grace God gives us (1 Peter 4:10). Proverbs tells us a wise person sees treasure and oil as precious, but a foolish man devours it (21:20). Paul continued the talk on stewardship in Romans 12:6–8. He exhorted us to prophesy, serve, teach, exhort, give, lead, and show mercy according to the grace given to us. In other words, to steward the grace.

We know the Lord expects us to wisely steward the gifts and talents He gives us based on the parable of the talents in Matthew 25. Jesus gave an illustration of a man who called his servants together to serve as stewards over his estate before he went on a long trip. He gave one five talents, one two talents, and another one talent. The first two were good stewards. The third man hid his talent in the ground. He did nothing to bring increase to what he was given. In the parable, the man rebuked the one who sat idly by with his talent in the ground, calling him a wicked and lazy steward. The talent he had was taken away and given to another.

In the conclusion of this parable, Jesus shared the lesson: "For to everyone who has, more will be given, and he will have abundance; but from him who does not have, even what he has will be taken away" (Matt. 25:29 NKJV). In the world of the prophetic—which includes the world of dreams and visions—we are responsible for stewarding the revelations or information we receive through this mode of communication.

God won't condemn us for being poor stewards, but we can certainly cause ourselves plenty of grief by failing to understand what God has been gracious enough to share. "It is the glory of God to conceal a matter, but the glory of kings is to search out a matter" (Prov. 25:2 NKJV). Part of stewarding your dream life is searching it out. But you can't properly search it out until you write down your dreams.

Write Down All Your Dreams

God expects us to be good stewards of everything He gives us—including our dreams. As with prophetic words, most of us will not remember every detail of our dreams days or months later—or even right after we have them. We've mentioned before that it's vital to write down your dreams immediately so you don't forget the details, because every detail matters. Although the Holy Spirit can certainly bring the details back to our remembrance, it's not good stewardship to rely on that when we are capable of taking steps to chronicle our dream life. And as I said, every detail matters. Leave nothing out that you can remember.

Here are two words of advice for you in the realm of recording your dreams: *don't wait*. Let me repeat those words: *don't wait*. Don't wait until a week later. Don't even wait until an hour after you wake up. Write down your dreams as soon as possible. The serious dreamer will keep a dream journal or a voice recorder—or at least a notepad and pen—on their nightstand so they can capture at least the outline of the dream before it is buried in sleep or the business of life.

Why am I stressing this again? The reality is you forget many of your dreams before you wake up and many others after you wake up—unless they were tied to strong emotions or unless the Lord gives you a special grace to remember or recall. Scientists argue about brain chemistry, and Christian dream experts point to the Devil distracting us. No one knows for sure why we so quickly forget our dreams. That's not important. The vital point here is if we do our part to write down or otherwise record a dream as soon as we can—or as soon as we wake up—we're demonstrating wise stewardship over our dream life, and we'll likely be given more dreams.

Write down *all* your dreams—even nightmares, even if you think they came from a good dose of Nyquil, even if they seem obscure or too whimsical to ever understand. You can judge the dream later. Right now, you simply record the evidence you'll later judge.

If you are like me, you don't want to wake up completely in

the middle of the night to record every detail of a dream. You can't afford to be exhausted the next day. That's okay. Write down some bullet points or record something with your phone. Just a few pieces of information will elicit most of the dream in the morning if you return to it immediately. It's especially important to write down any dialogue from a dream because that seems to be what we're most likely to forget. The overarching plot is typically easier to remember.

Many times, more revelation unfolds as you record and review your dreams—so capturing every detail for later review is even more vital. The dream may mean nothing to you right now, even after applying every interpretation tool available to you. God may hide the meaning until a later time. Writing down your dream now preserves the revelation so the Holy Spirit can bring it to your remembrance later. Writing it down is good stewardship.

Before we move on, here are some basics: Record the date of your dream. If you know the time, write that down too. Were you at home or in a hotel or at a friend's house when you had this dream? The location could be important. For example, the spiritual atmosphere around you could significantly impact your dreams. What was the context of your life when you had the dream? For example, were you going through a trial, celebrating a success, or grieving a loss? Record your emotional state and life events surrounding the dream. All these elements could help you judge the source of the dream, interpret the dream's meaning, or apply the dream's truths to your life.

Although you don't need to necessarily start interpreting the dream immediately after writing it down—you can if you have time—at least take a moment to write down any first impressions you may have about the dream's meaning. You may prove yourself wrong later, but that first impression could be a Holy Spirit impression, and you want to capture that before you forget.

Remember Your Dreams

Sometimes we know we had a significant dream but we cannot recall it. It happens to everybody. We have an inkling but can't articulate it. This can be especially frustrating.

First, understand that God could be hiding the revelation in your spirit only to open it up at a later time. He could be depositing a mystery in your heart—hiding it from the enemy—so that the Holy Spirit can bring it to your remembrance at exactly the right moment. Although you can't remember the dream now, you will immediately connect the dots when the Holy Spirit draws it from the well of your spirit and to your conscious mind.

"For God may speak in one way, or in another, yet man does not perceive it. In a dream, in a vision of the night, when deep sleep falls upon men, while slumbering on their beds, then He opens the ears of men, and seals their instruction. In order to turn man from his deed, and conceal pride from man" (Job 33:14–17 NKJV).

Other times we just have to press past a distracted mind or an enemy's assignment to keep the dream hidden. The simple exercise of writing down every little detail you can remember can open up the rest of the dream. Even recording your emotions after waking up can lead you back down that path. Another practical tip is to stop telling everyone, including yourself, that you can't remember your dreams. Your words contain the power of death and life (Prov. 18:21). You can kill your dream recall by continuing to confess doubt over your ability to remember.

When you first wake up in the morning, whether it's naturally, via a phone ringing, or by an alarm clock, don't immediately jump out of bed and start your day. Take a moment to pray and consider whether you had any dreams. Ask the Lord to bring dreams back to your remembrance before you go about your busy day. Being intentional about trying to remember is being a good steward and showing hunger to hear the Lord in this way.

I get up at the same time almost every day. I believe the routine of going to bed and getting up at the same time can help establish a sleep pattern that makes it more likely to remember your dreams. If you use an alarm, don't set it to wake you up with a blaring buzz—unless that's what it takes to rouse you—or to music. Sudden jarring noises or songs can interrupt your dream memory recall.

If you can remember even a little bit of a dream, sharing what you remember with a friend can help you recall more. There's something about communicating what we know that unlocks more revelation. And, by the way, the quality of your sleep can have an impact on your ability to remember. If you sleep too few hours or have poor sleep conditions—too hot, too cold, too bright, too noisy, too hungry—your mind will be distracted.

Judge Dreams According to Scripture

Before you spend a lot of time praying through, meditating, or interpreting a dream—and certainly before you seek to apply it to your life—it is important to judge the source of your dream. We discussed in an earlier chapter three broad sources of dreams: God, the enemy, and your carnal nature or flesh. But I want to remind you of a few practical keys to judging spiritual experiences taken from the principles in my book *Did The Spirit of God Say That? 27 Ways to Judge Prophecy.*

"Beloved, do not believe every spirit, but test the spirits, whether they are of God; because many false prophets have gone out into the world" (1 John 4:1 NKJV). I like the Amplified Classic translation of this verse, which reads: "Beloved, do not put faith in every spirit, but prove (test) the spirits to discover whether they proceed from God; for many false prophets have gone forth into the world."

Does anything in the dream violate Scripture? The Word and the Spirit always agree. The Holy Spirit inspired all Scripture (2 Peter 1:21). God does not contradict Himself. So, if the dream leads you away from the truth of the Bible or leads you into idolatry, it is not from God. Does the dream cause tormenting confusion in your soul? We know "God is not the author of confusion but of peace" (1 Cor. 14:33 NKJV).

Does the dream breed a spirit of fear in your heart? We know that "God has not given us a spirit of fear, but of power and of love and of a sound mind" (2 Tim. 1:7 NKJV). It's true that a dream from God can bring a fear of the Lord into your life. It's also true that God can show you something in a dream—a warning or some end-times events—that can shake you into prayer. But that's not the same as the spirit of fear.

Pray and ask the Lord to show you the source of the dream. If you can't discern it on your own, pray. You could also submit your dream to trusted spiritual advisors who can help you wade through the spiritual, natural, and emotional elements you may be experiencing. From a natural perspective, for example, if you're watching scary movies before you go to bed, it can affect your dreams. If you are going through a trial and experiencing swinging emotions, your subconscious may process that through your dreams.

On a very practical level, I've discovered that if God wants me to remember a dream, I just can't shake it. It seems the Holy Spirit just keeps bringing elements of the dream back to my memory, as if to spur me on to search out the meaning.

Pray Through Your Dreams

Once you've judged a dream to be accurate, it's time to exercise good stewardship by praying through the dream. I mentioned the need to pray through the dream and how to do it in an earlier chapter on interpretation. Being a good steward of a dream, however, isn't a "one and done" prayer session. There's a time to pray through a dream for revelation, then there's a time to pray through the dream to understand the application. Then again, there's a time to pray through the dream to build your faith in the face of the war against what God showed you.

Read through the dream as recorded in your journal. Although you may have interpreted large parts of your dream, as you read and pray it's possible to receive more revelation about what the Lord said or how to apply it. You may see things you did not see before or even remember parts of the dream you forgot. This exercise could unlock new spiritual insights and strategies that are vital to understanding or applying the dream.

As you pray through the dream, continue to come into agreement with the Lord's will. Ask Him to help you change from faith to faith and glory to glory. Ask Him to order your steps to the people and places that are relevant to the dream. Ask Him for wisdom on how to further interpret and apply the dream. Thank Him for speaking to you through this dream and invite Him to give you new dreams.

Picture Your Dreams

Stewarding your dream may include drawing the scenes from your dream or finding magazine pictures that resemble parts of your dream. Remember, dreams are a visual expression of communication. By feeding this visual aspect of the dream through sketches, painting, and other imagery, you are making the vision plain and keeping it before you (Hab. 2:2–3). The idea is to do anything that could help you gain more understanding or keep God's message fresh on your mind.

Meditate on Your Dreams

In the same way, it's critical to meditate on the dreams God gives you for ongoing revelation. Meditating on the Word of God will build your faith. Meditating isn't just for Buddhists or the New Agers. Meditation is God's idea: "This Book of the Law shall not depart from your mouth, but you shall meditate in it day and night, that you may observe to do according to all that is written in it. For then you will make your way prosperous, and then you will have good success" (Josh. 1:8 NKJV).

In Joshua 1:8, the Hebrew word for meditate is *hagah*. In the context of Joshua 1:8 and the application of God-given dream communications, it means "to utter, speak, devise, muse, imagine, utter." *Noah Webster's 1828 Dictionary* often offers definitions that reflect Scripture. Let's look at Webster's classic definition of meditate: "to think on; to revolve in the mind." Webster offers Psalm 1 as an example: "His delight is in the law of the Lord, and in His law doth he meditate day and night."

Share your dream with others, as wisdom dictates. Talk to God about it. Intentionally think about the colors, the scenery, the dialogue, the symbols, your emotions—all the interpretation elements of your dream. Also, meditate on any Scriptures in the dream or scriptural parallels. If God shows you a narrow gate in the dream, meditate on Matthew 7:13–14 NKJV: "Enter by the narrow gate; for wide is the gate and broad is the way that leads to destruction, and there are many who go in by it. Because narrow is the gate and difficult is the way which leads to life, and there are few who find it."

In terms of strategically stewarding your dream life, Mary's experience applies. When the three shepherds visited Joseph, Mary, and the baby Jesus after His birth, they shared with Mary many things the Lord told them about the child. I am sure it was overwhelming and hard to believe. But the Bible says, "Mary kept all these things and pondered them in her heart" (Luke 2:19 NKJV). The AMPC translation says, "Mary was keeping within herself all these things (sayings), weighing and pondering them in her heart."

Visualize Your Dreams

Don't let the New Agers steal the concept of visualization. Visualization is the formation of mental visual images. It is wrong to decide what you want, hold an image in your head, and think the universe is going to bring it to you. Any attempt to manipulate the mind is error. However, biblically, there's nothing wrong with seeing the dream again in your mind if the Lord brings it back. Likewise, you can think about what you saw and ask the Holy Spirit to help you see it again. While you want to avoid getting into your imagination and adding to the dream, with the Holy Spirit's guidance you can often see again what He showed you in a dream or a vision.

God created us with an imagination and seeing as true what the Word says is true is not a sin. You are healed in Christ. Seeing yourself healed is not wrong. It builds faith in the God who heals. God gives us His Word, and His Word can feed our holy imaginations to see as He sees. One of Paul's prayers illustrates this concept of seeing through the eyes of faith:

> That the God of our Lord Jesus Christ, the Father of glory, may give to you the spirit of wisdom and revelation in the knowledge of Him, the eyes of your understanding being enlightened; that you may know what is the hope of His calling, what are the riches of the glory of His inheritance in the saints, and what is the exceeding greatness of His power toward us who believe. (Eph. 1:17–19)

Here Paul mentions the "eyes" of our understanding. We know that our understanding does not have its own set of natural eyes. Rather, according to *The KJV New Testament Greek Lexicon*, *eyes* is a metaphor for "the eyes of the mind, the faculty for knowing." The word *understanding* in this verse means "the mind as a faculty of understanding, feeling, desiring; understanding; mind, i.e., spirit; way of thinking and feeling; and thoughts, either good or bad."

Essentially, Paul prayed that our spiritual eyes would be opened so we could see what God wants us to see. God created us to visualize. In fact, half of the human brain is devoted directly or indirectly to vision, according to an MIT study.[16] If I say the word *dog* right now, you would immediately think of a dog. What kind of dog you think of depends on many different factors that have shaped your experience.

Paul encouraged us to "set [our minds] on things above, not on things on the earth" (Col. 3:2 NKJV). Other translations say "think about" or "keep your minds on" or "set your sight on." The Greek word for *set* in this verse is *phroneo*, which means "to direct one's mind to a thing." When Jesus was on the cross, He kept His eyes on the prize (Heb. 12:1–2).

Let me be clear: there is potential for deception in visualization if you let your imagination run wild, out of check with the Spirit of God. Visualization in some inner healing practices troubles me. But if God has given you a dream or a vision and you think about what He showed you, this is no different than the concept of meditating on the logos or prophetic word of God. To refuse to think more or see again the images God showed you is to be a poor steward, neglecting to review or ponder communication you've received from the Lord.

Review Your Dream Journal

Review your dream journal at least annually to see if your dreams have a bearing on your reality, if there are recurring dreams, if the dreams already came to pass, and so on. You need to review your dreams for patterns and rhythms and understand there may be one revelation now and another revelation that applies to your life in the future.

CONCLUSION

20 Answers to Questions Every
Dreamer Wants to Know

A s I travel and teach on dreams, people consistently ask many of the same questions about the dream world. Some are easier to answer than others because we have Bible precedence or enough collective experience to offer a reliable theory. Other questions are more difficult to answer, but we can at least offer some godly advice. Still other questions are almost impossible to answer because of the subjectivity of the dream world or the sheer mysteries of God. I've included some of the most common questions I'm asked, along with answers I hope will be helpful.

1. What does it mean when I have the same dream over and over again?

Think about it this way. When you are growing up and your dad tells you the same thing over and over, what does it mean? Clearly, your dad is trying to get your attention. You didn't heed what he said the first time around or he would not have to keep repeating himself, right? He's either trying to get you to obey in an area where you are lacking obedience, he is warning you of some sort of danger, or he is reminding you of something important.

It's the same way with your heavenly Father. When God starts repeating Himself, whether through that still, small voice speaking to your heart, through Scriptures you seem to "randomly" stumble upon, through prophetic voices who prophesy the same words over and over with no knowledge of previous prophecies, or through dreams and visions, there's a sense of urgency in His heart for you to get the message.

The marketing world holds fast to what it calls the "rule of seven." This rule states that a prospect—a consumer—needs to see your marketing message at least seven times before they will ultimately take action and buy. Why seven times? One reason is because there's so much noise in the world—so many voices vying for our attention. Another reason is that we're all in a hurry. Our focus is often divided among many different things in today's multitasking world.

Psychologists tell you people repeat themselves because they don't feel they are being heard, because they are self-centered, or just because they love the sound of their voices. God is not self-centered, but He may choose to repeat Himself through various levels of prophetic communication because He doesn't feel He is really being heard. He knows when you hear Him. He doesn't want you to merely be a hearer of the Word either, because if you hear the Word and don't do the Word, you deceive yourself (James 1:22).

Put another way, God doesn't have to base your reception on His feelings. He knows when He's not being heard—and He wants you to hear Him because the message is vital to your life. "Indeed

God speaks once, or twice, yet no one notices it" (Job 33:14 NASB). Other translations say, "no one perceives it" (NIV) or "do not recognize it" (NLT) or "pays not attention" (New Heart English Bible) or "does not see" (Jubilee Bible 2000). I believe God, in His mercy and grace, repeats Himself so we'll get it.

After Moses died, God told Joshua four times (recorded in eighteen verses) to "be strong and courageous." Clearly, He was trying to strengthen Joshua for the battle ahead. Paul told the church at Philippi it was no trouble for him to write the same truths to them again (Phil. 3:1). Peter told his readers, "I consider it right, as long as I am in this earthly dwelling, to stir you up by way of reminder" (1 Peter 1:13 NASB).

When God gives you repetitious dreams, they may not be exactly alike but will contain similar elements, colors, names, or themes. It could be the same message played out in different dream codes that build on each other progressively, like chapters in a book or scenes in a movie. Think about it as when a pregnant woman's contractions increase. That signals the baby is coming soon. When God's frequency of dreams on a certain topic increase, God's urgency is increasing. Pay attention.

Also remember that God may give you a dream in one stage of your life that doesn't mean much. It's a seed He is planting in your heart so that you will have a confirmation when He gives you the next dream signaling a more imminent manifestation of His promise. I have had dreams of giving birth repeatedly in my life—long before entering into ministry. There came a time when others started having dreams about my giving birth, which marked an accelerated manifestation of His plans for me. Pay attention to repetition in dreams in your life as well as in dreams others have about you. There is purpose in the repetition.

2. I used to dream all the time. Why has my dream life suddenly ceased?

God is the giver of dreams. We can't decide to dream a God dream any more than we can decide to work a miracle because God is the Source of all miracles. It's up to Him to manifest the gift. Our part is to believe. With that in mind, there are at least two reasons why we go through times in our life when dreams are especially active and times when they suddenly cease.

First, God may choose to speak to us in a way other than the dream language. God speaks to us in many ways—through a still, small voice, through faint impressions, through an inner witness, through nature, or prophetic people, and so on. God wants us to learn the many ways He speaks to us so we become fluent in the language of the Holy Spirit. When we become familiar with God speaking to us through one mode of communication, sometimes He will switch it up to teach us another way of communication and to keep us pursuing His heart.

But there's another reason our dream lives may dry up. If we don't steward our dreams, God may choose to speak with us in a different way because He is full of grace and mercy and wants us to hear His message. If we're not writing down our dreams, meditating on our dreams, and seeking understanding of our dreams—if we're neglecting this mode of communication or mis-understanding what He is saying—He may choose to speak with us in a way we can grasp and reactivate our dream lives when we're mature enough to receive and understand what He is say-ing. God in His wisdom knows the best way to get His message across.

3. When do I share a dream I've received, and when do I keep it to myself?

First, let me say that the Lord has a purpose in everything. He will not show or tell you something about a person, city, nation—or even yourself—just so you can be "in the know." Knowledge God provides is never for knowledge's sake; it is to be applied. Doing nothing is never the right response.

Second, when the Lord gives you a dream, praying it through is never the wrong move. In other words, you can't go wrong praying. It may be that the Lord has called you to intercede based on your newfound knowledge from Him so that He can bring change to a situation or help a person in need. Prayer may not be the final action, but it's a good place to start.

I always tell people: The same Lord who gave you the dream will tell you what to do with it—*if you ask*. Don't sit and wonder what to do. Remember, the Lord didn't share His secrets with you so you could get puffed up with knowledge. He shared them so you could take action. *Ask the Lord!*

Wisdom asks the Lord before sharing a dream with others. Sharing what the Lord showed you might not edify, comfort, or exhort people. It might embarrass or make a person feel exposed or even angry. Remember when Joseph shared his dreams with his brothers? They got so angry they wanted to kill him and ultimately threw him into a pit and then sold him as a slave. If the Lord is showing you in a dream a weakness or need a person has, it may be that the Lord is showing you so that you can intercede for that person or come alongside to help without ever sharing the dream.

Again, when you have a dream, your first response should be

to inquire of the Lord, "Father, what do You want me to do with this knowledge? Do I share it with the people involved or pray on their behalf?" The same Lord who gave you the dream will tell you what to do with it. The Lord will give you an unction to prophesy. Without that unction, we should watch and pray and wait for the Lord's next instruction.

4. Can you have a dream within a dream?

Yes, you can have a dream within a dream. You can have a vision within a dream. You can have a trance within a dream. The dream world is virtually limitless because it exists beyond the confines of physical reality.

5. Is dream interpretation a special gift, or can anyone receive dream interpretations?

Just as there are those who have the gift of interpretation of tongues (1 Cor. 12), there are those who have the gift of interpreting dreams. The Bible specifically names two in the Old Testament: Joseph and Daniel. Let's look at the Scriptures.

In Genesis 41, Pharaoh was puzzled about a dream. None of his magicians could interpret it. Hearing Pharaoh's dilemma, the chief butler remembered how Joseph had accurately interpreted his and the butler's dreams while the three were in jail together. Joseph had a true gift in this area:

> Then Pharaoh sent and called Joseph, and they brought him quickly out of the dungeon; and he shaved, changed his

clothing, and came to Pharaoh. And Pharaoh said to Joseph, "I
have had a dream, and there is no one who can interpret it. But
I have heard it said of you that you can understand a dream, to
interpret it." (Gen. 41:14–15 NKJV)

Daniel had the gift of dream interpretation. Scripture calls
it out explicitly: "As for these four young men, God gave them
knowledge and skill in all literature and wisdom; and Daniel had
understanding in all visions and dreams" (Dan. 1:17 NKJV).

6. Can you receive impartations in your dreams?

The short answer is yes, but you can also receive dreams from the
enemy hoping to make you think you received an impartation. Paul
said: "For I long to see you, that I may impart to you some spiritual
gift, so that you may be established" (Rom. 1:11 NKJV). *Merriam-
Webster*'s dictionary defines *impart* as "to give, convey, or grant from
or as if from a store." Spiritually speaking, an impartation is a trans-
ference or an endowment of gifts or attributes. God is the one who
imparts to us in dreams. Consider this Scripture passage:

At Gibeon the Lord appeared to Solomon in a dream by
night; and God said, "Ask! What shall I give you?"
And Solomon said: "You have shown great mercy to Your
servant David my father, because he walked before You in truth,
in righteousness, and in uprightness of heart with You; You have
continued this great kindness for him, and You have given him
a son to sit on his throne, as it is this day. Now, O Lord my God,

You have made Your servant king instead of my father David, but I am a little child; I do not know how to go out or come in. And Your servant is in the midst of Your people whom You have chosen, a great people, too numerous to be numbered or counted. Therefore give to Your servant an understanding heart to judge Your people, that I may discern between good and evil. For who is able to judge this great people of Yours?"

The speech pleased the Lord, that Solomon had asked this thing. Then God said to him: "Because you have asked this thing, and have not asked long life for yourself, nor have asked riches for yourself, nor have asked the life of your enemies, but have asked for yourself understanding to discern justice, behold, I have done according to your words; see, I have given you a wise and under-standing heart, so that there has not been anyone like you before you, nor shall any like you arise after you." (1 Kings 3:4–12)

Did Solomon receive an impartation of God's wisdom in the dream? Yes, and God made sure we know this. After Solomon woke up, the next verses of Scripture reveal two women fighting over whose baby died and whose baby remained alive. Solomon offered such a wise judgment that this statement was recorded: "And all Israel heard of the judgment which the king had rendered; and they feared the king, for they saw that the wisdom of God was in him to administer justice" (1 Kings 3:28).

7. Can a dream from God make you fearful?

Inspired by the Holy Spirit, Paul wrote emphatically: "For God has not given us a spirit of fear, but of power and of love and of a sound mind" (2 Tim. 1:7 NKJV). Therefore, if a dream torments you, the dream was not from God because fear carries torment (1 John 4:18).

However, God can give you a dream that inspires a soberness or a fear of the Lord. He can show you things in your life you need to change that light a holy fire under you to take action. He may show you warnings of tragedy to come that put you on high alert. He can show you end-times dramas that, like John the revelator in the book of Revelation, you don't fully understand but leave you trembling.

If you feel fear, discern if it's a spirit of fear or the fear of the Lord to help you judge the dream. Before I move on, let's define the fear of the Lord by looking at some Greek and Hebrew words. One definition of the Hebrew word *yare* means "to fear, to respect, to reverence." The Greek word *phobos* can be translated "reverential fear." *Vine's Complete Expository Dictionary* defines it as "not a mere 'fear' of His power and righteous retribution, but a wholesome dread of displeasing Him." That's intense!

- The fear of the Lord is to hate evil (Prov. 8:13).
- The fear of the Lord is the beginning of wisdom (Prov. 9:10).
- The fear of the Lord is the beginning of knowledge (Prov. 1:7).
- The secret of the Lord is with those who fear Him (Ps. 25:14).
- There is no want for them who fear Him (Ps. 34:9).
- In the fear of the Lord, there is strong confidence and a fountain of life (Prov. 14:26–27).
- By the fear of the Lord are riches, honor, and life (Prov. 22:4).

8. Does God hide the interpretation of some dreams from the dreamer?

The Bible says the interpretation belongs to God (Gen. 40:8). At times, God gives us a dream and withholds part or all of the interpretation until a later time. As Paul put it, we see in part and we prophesy in part (1 Cor. 13:9). We can apply this Scripture loosely to the dream world, which is essentially God prophesying to us—or sending prophetic messages—through our dreams.

It's interesting to look at the Greek word for *know* in this verse. One definition of *ginosko* implies partial and growing knowledge. According to *The NAS New Testament Greek Lexicon*, it means "to learn to know, come to know, get a knowledge of, perceive, feel; to become known to know, understand, perceive, have knowledge of; to understand; to know."

The word *part* in this verse comes from the Greek word *meros*. According to the lexicon, it means "a part; a part due or assigned to one; lot, destiny; one of the constituent parts of a whole; in part, partly, in a measure, to some degree, as respects a part, severally, individually any particular, in regard to this, in this respect."

Sometimes when you can't seem to ascertain the interpretation of a dream, God is showing you things to come—things that will be confirmation at a later date and time—without giving you enough information to run out ahead of His timing. At times, the Lord is also giving you a heads-up of future events while leaving them hidden from the enemy. When the dream starts to come to pass, you'll discern the Lord's forewarning of the event, whether good or bad, and He will help you understand the meaning of the dream at that time.

This is somewhat like the mystery of praying in tongues. When we pray in our heavenly language, we speak mysteries to God. The enemy of our soul can't understand anything we're saying when we pray in the Spirit. We may not be willing to pray some things in our natural language we are praying in the Spirit. I'm convinced we're not only praying out our destinies at times, but praying what some would call the "scary prayers," like prayers to crucify our flesh or relationships that are hindering our growth. Most of the time we don't even understand what we're praying in the Spirit. But it's a perfect prayer and God understands every word.

There's also the reality that God can give you one level or layer of a dream interpretation now, but a deeper meaning months or years from now. In other words, dream revelations and interpretations can be progressive. There's not always firm meaning. That's another reason why it's so important to record your dreams and go back periodically to review what the Lord showed you in a dream and the understanding you gleaned at that time.

9. Can we control our dreams?

Some people argue they can control their dreams. Science-fiction plots and movies such as *Inception* like to glamorize this concept. But I submit to you if your dream is really from God, you can't control it. And why would you want to? If your dream is divinely suggested, then why would you want to manipulate it? I don't believe you can manipulate divinely suggested dreams.

10. Is my dream for me or someone else?

You are the subject of most of your dreams. Most of your dreams really are about you. God is speaking to you personally. If you are a prophet or an intercessor, you are more likely to have dreams about other people because God is giving you revelation for the purpose of prayer.

11. Why should I pay attention to my children's dreams?

"And it shall come to pass in the last days, says God, that I will pour out of My Spirit on all flesh; Your sons and your daughters shall prophesy, Your young men shall see visions, Your old men shall dream dreams" (Acts 2:17 NKJV).

Children dream—and children prophesy. We see this in the Bible. Consider these Scriptures: "Out of the mouth of babes and nursing infants You have ordained strength, because of Your enemies, that You may silence the enemy and the avenger" (Ps. 8:2 NKJV). And "Now this man had four virgin daughters who prophesied" (Acts 21:9 NKJV).

Children can say profound things—and have profound dreams. We should encourage our children to share their dreams and help them to seek the Lord for the interpretation.

12. What if I am sinning in my dream?

Many people have dreams they would never, ever dare share with anyone else because of the sinful nature of the dream. Can you sin in a dream? What you do in a dream is not real, so in that sense you can't sin in a dream. However, God can reveal sinful issues in your mind and emotions, such as anger, lust, or bitterness.

13. Should I pray for the gift of dream interpretation?

Yes, though it's ultimately up to the Lord if He chooses to give us this gift to exercise one time or permanently. Remember, the interpretation belongs to God (Gen. 40:8). Paul wrote, "Pursue love, and desire spiritual gifts, but especially that you may prophesy" (1 Cor. 14:1).

In 1 Corinthians 14:1, the word for *desire* in the Greek is *zeloo*. According to *The KJV New Testament Greek Lexicon*, it's a pretty intense feeling. It means: "to burn with zeal; in a good sense, to be zealous in the pursuit of good; desire earnestly; pursue." *Merriam-Webster*'s dictionary defines *zeal* as "a strong feeling of interest and enthusiasm that makes someone very eager or determined to do something."

14. Can I ask God to give me a dream if I am confused about what to do?

Yes, you can. You should seek God's face and tune your ear to His voice all the time. Sometimes, when we are walking through difficult trials, we don't trust our ability to hear God's voice. In times like these, I have asked the Lord to give me a dream and He has. Other times He hasn't. He's all-wise and knows what's best for us. I usually pray this type of prayer silently so the enemy doesn't hear me and try to bring me a false or deceptive dream. Keep in mind your soul could also give you a dream that does not reflect God's will. This is why it's important to discern the source of your dreams, as we discussed earlier in this book.

15. Why is it that when you speak with different dream interpreters they each have a different perspective on the same dream?

How do you determine which is the right one? What is the proper response to dreams? When seeking God for the interpretation of your dream, what questions should you ask?

16. What if I see repetitive numbers?

Sometimes God speaks to you through repeating numbers in dreams or even through natural life. Maybe everywhere you go, you're seeing 5:55. Could God be communicating triple grace? Maybe you see 11:11 all the time or have dreams with 11:11 in them. Could it be an impending transition?

It's possible. We have to ask the Lord what He is saying. Usually repetitive numbers—or anything repetitive—is God trying to get your attention. One strategy with numbers is to look up all the verses with the number sequences in the Bible. For example, if you see 5:34 everywhere, look up Genesis 5:34, Exodus 5:34, and so on throughout the Bible and see what strikes your spirit.

Be careful, though, not to read something into what's not there. We all have a reticular activating system. According to the *Textbook of Clinical Neurology*, "The reticular activating system (RAS) is a network of neurons located in the brain stem that project anteriorly to the hypothalamus to mediate behavior, as well as both posteriorly to the thalamus and directly to the cortex for activation of awake, desynchronized cortical EEG patterns."[17]

That's fancy scientific language, but the outcome of this activating system is when you are in the market, let's say, for a red Honda you'll start seeing red Hondas everywhere. By the same token, once you pick up on 11:11, you might start noticing 11:11 everywhere. Is it really God showing you this, or is your RAS just making you hypersensitive to it? Remember, the interpretation belongs to God (Gen. 40:8). Ask Him.

17. What does it mean if I see people in my dreams who have already passed away?

In most cases, seeing someone who has passed away in your dream is a familiar spirit, which we discussed earlier in the book. "For the living know that they will die; But the dead know nothing, and they have no more reward, for the memory of them is forgotten" (Eccl. 9:5).

Remember when David's son conceived with Bathsheba died? David explicitly said, "But now he is dead; why should I fast? Can I bring him back again? I shall go to him, but he shall not return to me" (2 Sam. 12:23 NKJV). The New Living Translation of that verse says, "the departed spirit shall not return."

The manifestation of dead people in dreams and visions is a controversial topic in the body of Christ. Some would argue they are not dead if they are in Christ because they are still alive—their bodies gave way to mortality, but their spirits are immortal. But often when dead people appear in dreams, they are familiar spirits. I will not go so far as to say there are not exceptions. God can use someone who has passed away to symbolize something or someone else in a dream. It becomes dangerous, I believe, when dead people start bringing you messages in dreams. You have to judge the source of the dream, which we discussed earlier in the book.

18. Where does déjà vu fit into the world of dreams?

Déjà vu is a French phrase that means "already seen." *Merriam-Webster* defines déjà vu as "the illusion of remembering scenes and events when experienced for the first time" and "feeling that one has seen or heard something before" and "something overly or unpleasantly familiar."

I've experienced this many times—and you probably have too. About two-thirds of the population reports déjà vu experiences, according to a report in *Current Directions in Psychological Science*. But the scientific world can't settle on the root of déjà vu.

According to research, déjà vu can come from mental disorders, such as anxiety, dissociative identity disorder, or schizophrenia. Déjà vu can also come from medical disorders like epilepsy, and some pharmaceutical drugs can cause this "already seen" experience.

Other researchers point to memory-based origins. *Psychology Today* offered three reasons for déjà vu: (1) the result of some sort of "mismatch" in how we're simultaneously sensing and perceiving the world around us; (2) a fleeting malfunctioning between the long-and short-term circuits in the brain; and (3) a region of the brain called the rhinal cortex, involved in detecting familiarity, may be inexplicably activated without actually activating memory (hippocampal) circuits.

Some prophetic people point to déjà vu as a deep prophetic experience. Could it be possible that God is using what feels like déjà vu to communicate His truths? Or is it a familiar spirit? Is it witchcraft? God can bring dreams back to your memory and it may feel like déjà vu but it's not—it's God bringing it back to your memory.

Some prophetic people argue déjà vu is always from God. I don't believe that any more than I believe every dream we have is from God. In fact, déjà vu could be demonic.

Déjà vu is mentioned nowhere in the Bible, but one thing is certain: it is not a spiritual gift. This is not the gift of prophecy. It's not the word of knowledge. Scripture is very clear that some supernatural communications and expressions come from God's Spirit (1 Cor. 12:4–11), while others come from evil forces (Deut. 18:10–12).

Could what feels like déjà vu be God showing you something? Possibly. But given its connection to witches and the paranormal, the concept of déjà vu does not belong in a prophetic person's spiritual vocabulary of God expressions. At best, it's likely a similar memory that's buried in your subconscious. At worst, it's witchcraft.

19. What if you are someone else in a dream? For example, you seem to be in the person's body, or you look like the person but it's really you.

Appearing as someone else in a dream could signify the Lord is showing you what it is like to walk in that person's shoes. This is a good indication that you are being positioned to intercede for them or minister to them with greater empathy. It could also mean that you are in conflict with this person and the Lord wants you to understand how they are viewing the conflict so you can resolve it.

20. Why do the dreams I remember usually take place around 3:00 a.m.?

In Israel, they had what were called watches. There are eight prayer watches in three-hour periods. We won't go into a full-blown teaching on watches here, but waking up at 3:00 a.m. with dreams could be significant, especially if you are having spiritual warfare or intercessory prayer dreams. The 3:00 a.m. to 6:00 a.m. watch is the fourth watch and is when demons are most active. Jesus walked on water during the fourth watch during a storm (Matt. 14:25–33). It's known by prayer warriors as a time to declare God's Word and command your morning.

A PRAYER OVER YOUR DREAM LIFE

This book has taken you on a journey through the biblical world of dreams—and their unique meaning to you. By now you should have no doubt God speaks to people in dreams and has spoken to you in your dreams over the years. You've discovered how to discern the source of your dreams, dream classifications, scriptural, subjective, and cultural dream codes, and more.

What now? Commit to being a good steward of your divinely suggested dreams. Determine to strategically steward your dream life. I encourage you to set aside some time to think about the dreams you've had in days, months, and years past. Write down any dreams you remember—dreams you haven't been able to shake—and use the principles in this book, along with prayer, to unlock your dream codes.

Going forward, put the information you've learned in this book to good use each and every time you have a dream. Don't relent on searching out the meanings of your God-given dreams.

Your dreams matter. Remember, "It is the glory of God to conceal a matter, but the glory of kings is to search out a matter" (Prov. 25:2). Search with sincerity and God won't let you miss any important messages or meanings in your dream life.

I sincerely hope you have already seen an increase in your dream life and have gained clarity on dream meanings from your past and present even while reading this book. If you haven't started dreaming yet or want to dream more—or if you still just can't wrap your mind around what God's Spirit is saying, I want to offer you this prayer outline. Pray it in faith. Pray it often. And believe God for the answers.

Use the following prayer to help activate your dream life:

Father, in the name of Jesus, I thank You that I hear Your voice. I thank You that You speak to me in many different ways. God, please help me hear You in Your many expressions, whether that still, small voice, faint impressions, visions, or dreams. Give me dreams at night in which Your will is revealed to me.

Lord, I stand now in faith and take authority over any and all dream killers in my life. I command blockages, hindrances, attacks, or perversions of my dream life to be broken now, in Jesus' name. I break the power of insomnia. I break nightmares, night terrors, sleep paralysis, and other enemy assignments against my dreams. I come against every assignment to steal my dreams, cause me not to remember them, or to misinterpret and misapply them.

Father, help me to press into what You are saying. Help me to never take Your dream-inspired messages lightly but to be a good steward of them. Teach me how to understand what You are saying to me in my sleep. Help me not to rely too much on my own wisdom or the wisdom of others either through personal counsel or dream interpretation books but to seek You first. Remind me continually that the interpretation belongs to You. In Jesus name, Amen.

Acknowledgments

I'm grateful to John and Vanessa Angelini, Austin and Sierra Holmes, and my team of intercessors at the Awakening House of Prayer, as well as those at PrayforJennifer.com and *Mornings with the Holy Spirit* prophetic prayer broadcasts. You helped pray the grace on me to write this book with fresh revelation and godly wisdom. Thank you for your faithful prayers. I'm grateful to Mike Briggs, Woodley Auguste, and, of course, Joel Kneedler and his team at Emanate Books for believing with me that dreams are such a vital topic in this hour and for working with me to publish what I believe is going to be handbook for today's Christian dreamers. Thank you all for your commitment to seeing the will of the Lord come to pass.

NOTES

1. Abné M. Eisenberg Ph.D., *Welcome to My Mind* (Trafford Pub., 2013), 270.
2. John W. Price, interview on radio, *Engines of Our Ingenuity*.
3. Emil G. Hirsch, Solomon Schechter, Ludwig Blau, Cyrus Adler, and Joseph Jacobs, "Dreams," Jewish Encyclopedia.com, http ://www.jewishencyclopedia.com/articles/5311-dreams.
4. "National Sleep Foundation's sleep time duration recommendations: methodology and results summary," *Sleep Health Journal of the National Sleep Foundation*, March 2015, Volume 1, Issue 1, pages 40–43.
5. Rev. Joseph Benson, *The New Testament of Our Lord and Saviour Jesus Christ* (University of Michigan, 1854, digitized Feb. 17, 2006), 230a.
6. William Smith, Smith's Bible Dictionary, entry for "trance."
7. Maria B. Woodworth, *Life and Experience of Maria B. Woodworth*, Revival Library, http://www.revival-library.org/index.php /catalogues-menu/pentecostal/life-and-experience-of-maria -b-woodworth.
8. *Nave's Topical Bible*, biblehub.com/topical/naves/v/vision--a _mode_of_revelation.htm.
9. *Gill's Exposition of the Entire Bible*.
10. *Benson Commentary*.

11. "Sleep Paralysis," webmd.com.

12. "How Often Do We Dream?" Sleep.org, powered by National Sleep Foundation, https://sleep.org/articles/how-often-dreams/.

13. "Facts About Dreaming," https://www.webmd.com/sleep-disorders /guide/dreaming-overview#1.

14. Adi Robertson, "Where Do Dreams Come From? Fewer Places Than You'd Expect," The Verge, April 3, 2015, https://www .theverge.com/2015/4/3/8337427/rat-rem-sleep-brain-activity-study.

15. Institute for Health and Human Potential; EQ or EI.

16. "Pillow-Talk," January 22–26, 2011, http://web.media.mit .edu/~vmb/papers/4p375-portocarrero.pdf.

17. ScienceDirect, https://www.sciencedirect.com/topics/neuroscience /reticular-activating-system.

About the Author

Jennifer LeClaire is an internationally recognized author, conference speaker, and prophetic voice. She is the senior leader of several prayer networks, including Awakening House of Prayer, Ignite Network, and the Awakening Blaze prayer movement. Jennifer formerly served as the first female editor of *Charisma* magazine and has authored more than twenty-five books, including *Mornings with the Holy Spirit*, *The Making of a Prophet*, and *The Spiritual Warrior's Guide to Defeating Jezebel*. She is a frequent contributor to two of *Charisma*'s publications, the *Prophetic Insight* newsletter, and her very own column "The Plumb Line," in addition to her frequent contributions to the Elijah List. Jennifer lives in Fort Lauderdale, Florida, and is active online via Facebook, Twitter, and YouTube.

Please visit her ministry website: www.jenniferleclaire.org.